The Violence of Being

The Violence of Being

Prophetic Writings, 2016

JEFF HOOD

RESOURCE *Publications* · Eugene, Oregon

THE VIOLENCE OF BEING
Prophetic Writings, 2016

Copyright © 2017 Jeff Hood. All rights reserved. Except for brief quotations in critical publications or reviews, no part of this book may be reproduced in any manner without prior written permission from the publisher. Write: Permissions, Wipf and Stock Publishers, 199 W. 8th Ave., Suite 3, Eugene, OR 97401.

Resource Publications
An Imprint of Wipf and Stock Publishers
199 W. 8th Ave., Suite 3
Eugene, OR 97401

www.wipfandstock.com

PAPERBACK ISBN: 978-1-5326-1716-4
HARDCOVER ISBN: 978-1-4982-4165-6
EBOOK ISBN: 978-1-4982-4164-9

Manufactured in the U.S.A.   FEBRUARY 17, 2017

For Dillard

Jesus is not for sale!

Who talked about #BarbaraDawson in church this morning? Jesus can't breathe. #BlackLivesMatter

So long to one of the queerest of them all . . . #DavidBowie. I'll see you in heaven.

"Either Sheriff Lupe Valdez releases the names of the deputies who killed Joseph Hutcheson or we need to release her from her job."

"Death to the death penalty!"

"The people of Dallas County have a right to know who they're encountering when they go into this lobby . . . "

Does anyone else still question why I hate religious institutions?

God is still here and She is not silent.

"God is an energy that magically flows within all that is around us."

Proud to stand with fellow activists and block the #Dallas #MLKDAY Parade to protest police brutality. #NoJusticeNoPeace.

"#ChristopherBrooks was executed earlier tonight. Now, #Alabama will have to deal with the consequences of killing one of God's children." #deathpenalty

I'm convinced that the Palestinians remain the most oppressed people on the face of our planet. #StoptheOppression #EndtheOccupation #BoycottIsrael

"Jesus' revolution is not safe. Let us pray that the future will belong to those who love dangerously."

"Though the work is slow, I believe the death penalty is on the way out . . . Until then, I just try to be present." #deathpenalty #justice #God

You will find God when you realize that God was never lost. #theology

This is what a spontaneous first #Spokenword performance looks like . . . The Judas Remix

Those consumed with saving the institutional church should consider it was never the church to begin with. #universal

If you're curious about his absence at #church this morning, Jesus stayed home with everyone else who's tired of going.

"This is the blood of Jesus Christ."

"Due to your promotion of the ordination of women, I can look around and say that God is with us in all her splendor. Hallelujah!"

Zimbabwe is an amazingly beautiful country to write in.

When you carry a gun, everything is a potential target.

Thanks for everything dear friend. #HarperLee

"Unless God is Queer . . . God is not God."

Certainty is the greatest enemy of God. #doubt

There is something so spiritual about #chickens.

Back on death row. #abolition

"Jesus is so much bigger than Matthew, Mark, Luke or John."

Chicken Farmer.

Women make the world turn. #IWD2016

Consequences shouldn't dictate our faith, our faith should dictate the consequences.

Busyness is not the measure of a human . . . love is. #sundayschool

Don't stop pushing toward the light.

Righteousness not ease must drive us into our future.

The police are out of control. Jesus stands with those who stand up to such brutality. #JoseCruz #BrownLivesMatter

Terror is the antithesis of God. Let's pray for more God and less Terror. #Brussels

"I intend to conduct 'an act of civil disobedience' during the execution." #execution #deathpenalty #Texas

"I plan to get arrested tonight in Huntsville, protesting the execution of convicted murderer Adam Ward." #execution #HolyWeek #deathpenalty #Texas

"God commands disobedience in the midst of these executions." #Texas #deathpenalty

"Obedience to our faith requires civil disobedience." #DeathPenalty #HolyWeek #Jesus #Texas

"I want my children to look back and see the pictures from the arrest and say, 'My father did all that he could do to keep the State of Texas from killing people.'" #HolyWeek #Texas

I don't believe in death without resurrection. #Easter

"I'm certain that if the sheriff had her way we still wouldn't have these names." #Dallas #Texas #JosephHutcheson

Our God has expired and we need a new one with some relevancy. #theology

The most spiritual moments of my life never take place in churches. #FreeSpirituality

Grace is as much about failure as it is about mercy. #gospel

Jesus isn't a Christian. #gospel

Communion.

Churches that cannot afford childcare cannot afford the young families they need to survive.

13.1 Miles Later.

I don't believe in our churches. I believe in our Jesus.

I don't believe that the Bible is the Word of God. I only believe that the Word of God is the Word of God.

"Art is the living Word of God."

Compromise is always the greatest enemy of truth.

Those who talk about homelessness the most usually care the least about the cause of it.

My flock. #chickens

"I thank God for #Prince. The funk is gone."

The morning haul. #chickens

Spent today with the consummate theologian, Dr. Cornel West.

"Unbind our souls oh God!"

We are more than our understanding.

Saint Daniel Berrigan RIP

Texas Death Row inmate Paul Storey is a child of God and I'm so proud to serve as his spiritual advisor.

There is no such thing as a good person . . . or a bad one for that matter. #theology

"Behold, I stand at the bathroom door and knock . . . "-Jesus #FreethePee

The eye of the Rooster.

Emily. Mom.

We ARE abolishing the death penalty.

God is not normal. #queer

We will never get today back. Stand for justice. #theology

"I guarantee you that Malcolm X has taught me more about God than 99.99% of the Christian ministers I've met."

"Masculinity is a lie from the pits of hell. Quit trying to be a man and just be."

US Supreme Court: THE DEATH PENALTY IS RACIST. Who will be the last person to die for the lie that we can teach people not to to kill by killing?

"People are celebrated when they don't get too far ahead. Beware of those who celebrate you. They might be the ones holding you back the most."

"Loving your neighbor doesn't include killing them."

God just got knocked out. #Ali

"Every step we take draws us closer to the day when there will be no death penalty!"

"Imagine what would have happened over the course of a year if those young girls at the pool here in McKinney had been white. Even though justice is late, we're not going to let justice be denied!"

"If your church doesn't discuss this tragedy today, you need to find a new church." #Pulse #Orlando

How can any church exclude LGBTQ people after this? #Orlando #Pulse

You can't follow Jesus with a gun in your hand.

"The fact that there wasn't a legal indictment in this case doesn't mean that the Dallas County Sheriff's Department isn't under a moral indictment for killing Joseph Hutcheson."

Two children close to the age of my five children will grow up without a mother over politics. What the hell is wrong with us? #JoCox

The greatest title I will ever know is DAD. #grateful

What is wrong with us? These agents should be fired immediately.

"The Fellowship of Reconciliation USA is the peace movement perfected."

MURDER in Baton Rouge! GOD is NOT MOCKED! #AltonSterling #BlackLivesMatter

"Stop Shooting America!" #BatonRouge

Make no mistake, Jesus stands with the unarmed benevolent caretaker of an autistic boy who had his hands up and got shot by the police anyway. #disturbing

"I think people are ready for love and justice. I think we have to figure out what we can do to make that happen."

"The world was in chaos." #Dallas

"Amid the dangers of our world, let's take the opportunity to open our doors and meet with each other. Let us put aside differences and dialogue . . . Then, let us march forward together in the unity of justice. Is progress not what our civil liberties are for?" #Dallas

God is in us.

We are a people standing in the need of prayer. #SundaySchool

Conformity is the great destroyer of the God within us. / aka Don't conform.

Jesus always stands with the oppressed. #Charlotte #Tulsa

"Every time I come down here, I remember that five people were shot and killed down here.." #Dallas

Jesus didn't come wrapped. The most important things in life usually don't. #Christmas

Terror in Turkey. May 2017 be the year we overcome fundamentalism in all its forms. #Istanbul

Contents

January 3, 2016	Killing Andrew Thomas | 1
January 3, 2016	Sheikh Nimr al-Nimr Lives! : A Word to Christians | 4
January 6, 2016	The Sad Case of Dr. Larycia Hawkins | 5
January 8, 2016	Repent! Follow Jesus! : A Plea for Radicalism | 6
January 10, 2016	The God in the Table | 9
January 11, 2016	Barbara Dawson: A Child of God Slaughtered by Medical Capitalism and Our Police State | 11
January 13, 2016	Dallas Celebrates the White Dr. Martin Luther, King, Jr. | 13
January 16, 2016	True Pastors Don't Endorse Candidates! | 14
January 18, 2016	The Thingyness of God | 16
January 19, 2016	Release the Names! : An Address to the Dallas County Commissioners Court | 18
January 20, 2016	I Believe in IT : The God Beyond God | 20
January 20, 2016	The Case of Richard Masterson | 22
January 21, 2016	The Incarnation of Jesus . . . Anthony Hill | 24
January 25, 2016	Presence is the Antidote to Killing | 25
January 25, 2016	What Does God Look Like? | 27
January 26, 2016	Jesus: "Fuck the Police" | 29
January 26, 2016	Tonight, We Were Dining with God. | 31
January 29, 2016	The Crime Was Horrible | 32
January 31, 2016	The Shirt | 33

Contents

February 3, 2016	Government Should be Afraid of Christians / A Word from Zimbabwe | 34
February 4, 2016	The Mentally Ill of Zimbabwe | 35
February 5, 2016	The Chickens | 37
February 6, 2016	The Impromptu Sermon : Thoughts of Christian Defiance in Zimbabwe | 39
February 7, 2016	The Mentally Ill God: A Sermon from Zimbabwe | 41
February 7, 2016	Baptist Colors in Zimbabwe | 44
February 8, 2016	Resisting Mugabe in Zimbabwe | 45
February 9, 2016	Where is Itai? : Thoughts on a Disappeared Man in Zimbabwe | 47
February 10, 2016	The Ashes: A Celebration in Zimbabwe | 49
February 11, 2016	Zimbabwe Sleeping | 51
February 12, 2016	Beauty: The Sunset Revelation | 52
February 13, 2016	Lenten Remix 1: The Fluid John 3:16 | 53
February 13, 2016	Lenten Remix 2: The Simple Great Commission | 54
February 14, 2016	Lenten Remix 3: Jesus on Truth | 55
February 14, 2016	Lenten Remix 4: The Greatest of These | 56
February 15, 2016	Lenten Remix 5: Love in Rome | 57
February 15, 2016	Boycott the Cooperative Baptist Fellowship! | 58
February 16, 2016	Lenten Remix 6: I Never Left | 62
February 17, 2016	Lenten Remix 7: NO Beginning | 63
February 17, 2016	Lenten Remix 8: The Dying God. | 64
February 19, 2016	Lenten Remix 9: The Screaming Christ | 65
February 20, 2016	Lenten Remix 10: The Ass Stones | 66
February 20, 2016	Save Andrew Thomas. | 67
February 21, 2016	Lenten Remix 11: End Racism | 68
February 22, 2016	Lenten Remix 12: Give Your Life | 69
February 23, 2016	Lenten Remix 13: I Got This | 70
February 24, 2016	Lenten Remix 14: Don't Worry | 71
February 25, 2016	Lenten Remix 15: Just Be Love | 72
February 26, 2016	Lenten Remix 16: Jesus Had a Vagina | 73
February 27, 2016	Lenten Remix 17: Jesus Brought the Wine | 74
February 28, 2016	Lenten Remix 18: Loving Your Enemy | 75
February 29, 2016	Lenten Remix 19: The Fake Jesus | 76

Contents

March 1, 2016	Lenten Remix 20: Fuck It	77
March 2, 2016	Lenten Remix 21: The Loving End	78
March 3, 2016	Lenten Remix 22: Hate Money!	79
March 4, 2016	Lenten Remix 23: Female Disciples	80
March 5, 2016	Lenten Remix 24: The Genitalia of Jesus	81
March 6, 2016	Lenten Remix 25: The Old Testament is Often No Testament	82
March 6, 2016	Boycott the Cooperative Baptist Fellowship! // Uncensored	83
March 6, 2016	Madeleine/Lucas: A Poem	87
March 7, 2016	Lenten Remix 26: The Flood	89
March 8, 2016	Lenten Remix 27: Politicians Killed Jesus	90
March 9, 2016	Lenten Remix 28: Seek God	91
March 10, 2016	Lenten Remix 29: Beyond Nations	92
March 11, 2016	Chicken S*it Pastors	93
March 12, 2016	Lenten Remix 30: The Idolatry of Consequences & Donald Trump	94
March 13, 2016	Lenten Remix 31: Hell Exists and It's Here	95
March 14, 2016	Lenten Remix 32: Politics is Not Our Faith	96
March 15, 2016	Lenten Remix 33: Jesus Didn't Have to Die	97
March 16, 2016	Lenten Remix 34: The Nocturnal Emissions of Jesus	98
March 16, 2016	When a Black Cop Kills an Unarmed Child	99
March 17, 2016	Lenten Remix 35: The Heresy of Conversation	101
March 18, 2016	Lenten Remix 36: The Money Changers	102
March 20, 2016	Letter to the Editor Before the Execution of Adam Ward	103
March 21, 2016	The Blood: A Holy Week Execution	105
March 21, 2016	Crazy Like Me: A Holy Week Execution	108
March 23, 2016	Lenten Remix 37: Jesus is the Stranger	110
March 23, 2016	Lenten Remix 38: Dying	111
March 23, 2016	Lenten Remix 39: Jesus is Hungry	112
March 23, 2016	Lenten Remix 40: Living	113
March 24, 2016	The Resurrection of Ms. Shade Schuler	114

Contents

April 7, 2016	A Powerful Word | 116
April 8, 2016	The Execution: In Pragmatic Verse | 117
April 9, 2016	Fifty Years after the Death of God: Learning to Kill | 118
April 10, 2016	Memories | 121
April 22, 2016	Her name is Amy Francis-Joyner | 122
April 24, 2016	Max Soffar is Alive and We're Dead | 123
April 25, 2016	The Last Verdict: A Book Review | 125
May 8, 2016	My Flock | 127
May 8, 2016	no surrender : an ode to Emily | 130
May 22, 2016	From the Party | 132
May 26, 2016	The Dream: A Vision of Our Reality | 134
May 27, 2016	The Slap | 136
May 28, 2016	The United States Flag at the Front of the Church is Blasphemous | 137
May 29, 2016	A Memorial Day Prayer | 140
June 1, 2016	The Death of Heroes and The Divinity of Difference | 141
June 2, 2016	On Silence | 143
June 4, 2016	God Isn't the Cure | 144
June 7, 2016	Stop With the Damn Resolutions | 147
June 8, 2016	Hillary Clinton is the AntiChrist | 148
June 9, 2016	On Conflict: Conversations with a Disciple | 152
June 11, 2016	Learning to Die/Fly | 154
June 12, 2016	Christians are the Real Terrorists | 156
June 13, 2016	Move Your Ass | 158
June 14, 2016	On Tomorrow: Conversations with a Disciple | 159
June 17, 2016	On the One Year Anniversary of the Tragedy at Mother Emanuel AME Church | 160
June 18, 2016	On the 10th Anniversary of My Ordination | 161
June 18, 2016	The Beyond Stunning Hypocrisy of the Cooperative Baptist Fellowship | 163
June 20, 2016	The Gospel Next Door | 165
June 20, 2016	We're Dead: Guns Mattered More | 166
June 24, 2016	Dialogues with a Disciple: On the Ocean | 168
June 25, 2016	The Cost of Your Plate | 169

Contents

June 26, 2016	The Passion of Charles Moore: Two Years Later | 170
June 27, 2016	The Tall Grass | 173
June 29, 2016	Cracked Eyes | 175
June 30, 2016	United Methodist Insensitivity Unleashed in North Texas | 177
July 2, 2016	Spiritual Discipline is Spiritual Destruction | 179
July 4, 2016	The Day After the 4th | 182
July 16, 2016	Now | 184
July 18, 2016	Babel. | 185
July 20, 2016	City Council. | 188
July 24, 2016	Future | 189
July 26, 2016	The Passion of Jacques Hamel | 190
July 29, 2016	The Absence of Peace | 191
July 30, 2016	Don't Go To Church. Be The Church. | 195
August 4, 2016	Relearning to Think: Thoughts from Dallas | 196
August 18, 2016	Curbing Our Free Speech | 199
August 19, 2016	Jeff Wood Letter | 202
August 31, 2016	The Sunday Existentialist | 204
September 1, 2016	Sidewalk Hate | 207
September 2, 2016	The One Question that Defines Our Faith | 208
September 3, 2016	Problems. | 209
September 4, 2016	Listen. We keep hearing of pain and rumors of pain. | 210
September 6, 2016	Those Confederate Flags in De Leon | 211
September 7, 2016	Dallas is Still in Denton | 213
September 22, 2016	Words for the Enough is Enough Rally | 215
September 24, 2016	Staying Home: Churcholm Syndrome | 216
September 25, 2016	Bart Ate God | 218
September 27, 2016	Dreams. | 219
September 28, 2016	Prayer at the Conclusion of Shane Claiborne in North Texas | 221
September 30, 2016	Forgive Us Marksville: #JeremyMardis | 222
October 2, 2016	The Last Person to Die for a Lie | 223
October 3, 2016	Denton Dinning with 5 Children | 226
October 5, 2016	Voices of Love. | 228

Contents

October 5, 2016	Allahu Akhbar	229
October 6, 2016	Missing Dreams	230
December 12, 2016	The Absent God	231
December 12, 2016	Christmas Everywhere	233
December 13, 2016	War Crimes in Aleppo: Do Something!	234
December 13, 2016	His Name is Francisco Serna	235
December 14, 2016	The Death of Truth	236
December 15, 2016	Pray for Dylann Roof	237
December 16, 2016	The God Beyond God	238
December 17, 2016	Born to Be Murdered? : A Word from Bethlehem	239
December 19, 2016	Murder in Ankara : The Perpetual Crucifixion	241
December 23, 2016	Forbidden Words: Christmas Interactions with the Queer Christ	242
December 26, 2016	The End of Memory is The Beginning of God	251
December 30, 2016	Is the Slaughter of the Innocent the Slaughter of God?	252

JANUARY 3, 2016

Killing Andrew Thomas

On a frequent basis, I get messages from death row inmates. Due to the volume of my work, I can only engage a small percentage of those who write. In early November, I received a request for help from Tennessee. Opening the envelope, I figured Andrew Thomas would get my regrets. I was wrong. Before I finished the note, there was a phrase at the top of the letter that caught my eye, "I'm innocent." It was not that I hadn't heard such talk before. I can assure you that anyone who does this work hears claims of innocence on a regular basis. This time was different. Line by line, I found his story more and more compelling. Sensing a grave injustice, I was desperate to know more.

The road went on forever. Darkness grew. Exhaustion set in. If I was going to make it, I had to drive faster. Nashville was much further than I anticipated. When I arrived at the prison, I went straight in. Minutes later, I was ushered into the visitation space. Upon entering, Andrew Thomas embraced me with a hug. Surprised by the welcome, I looked Andrew in the eye and asked him to tell me everything. I believe he did.

On April 21, 1997, armored car guard James Day picked up deposits at a Walgreens in Memphis, Tennessee. Upon exiting the store, Day met an assailant who robbed and shot him. Jumping in a white car, the shooter was driven from the scene by another person. Authorities recovered the abandoned vehicle down the road. On July 21, 1997, Bobby Jackson attempted to rob an armored car at Southbrook Mall.

Upon arrest, Jackson admitted that this was not the first time he sought to or successfully robbed an armored car. One of the witnesses in the Walgreens robbery identified Jackson as the driver of the getaway car. Also around this time, Andrew Thomas and Anthony Bond were arrested on unrelated charges. Investigators determined that Bond's fingerprints matched prints on the getaway car from the Walgreens robbery. When confronted with this information, Bond admitted to being the getaway driver in the Walgreens robbery and claimed that Andrew was his accomplice and Day's shooter. Immediately, Andrew denied involvement. Andrew didn't match any of the descriptions provided by witnesses. Though Bobby Jackson was a heavy man and had a history or robbing armored cars in the area, authorities pursued Andrew as their primary suspect. In the midst of a rush to wrap up the case, Bond cut a deal with federal prosecutors for a lighter sentence and agreed to testify against Andrew. Based on Bond's testimony, Andrew was convicted and sentenced to life for the Walgreens robbery.

James Day died on October 2, 1999. Though Day suffered from heart disease, high blood pressure, diabetes and obesity, the Shelby County Medical Examiner Dr. O.C. Smith ruled the death a homicide related to the gunshot of two and a half years earlier. The State of Tennessee put Andrew Thomas and Anthony Bond on trial for murder and sought the death penalty. Bond pled out and got life. The testimony of Andrew's estranged wife Angela Jackson was the key factor in his conviction. During the trial, Jackson gave detailed accounts of Andrew's purported confession and distribution of the stolen money. In addition to having dated Bobby Jackson, Jackson was also involved in a bitter divorce with Andrew at the time. In an unimaginable breach of legal ethics, prosecutors paid Jackson $750 for her testimony. Richard Fischer was the only person to put Andrew at the scene. Revealingly, Fischer falsely identified two men before he identified Andrew. Not long after he was convicted and sentenced to die, Andrew received a letter from Anthony Bond. On numerous handwritten pages, Bond admitted that he partnered with Angela Jackson to falsely implicate Andrew. Though it seems more *than likely that Anthony Bond and Bobby Jackson are the actual culprits in the Walgreens robbery, Andrew Thomas is the only one the State of Tennessee is trying to kill.*

When he finished his story, Andrew passed me a napkin that read, "I am innocent." I was moved. Before he could ask, I told Andrew that I would stand with him and do all that I could to save his life. The guard informed us that our time was up. Leaning in and putting my arm around my brother, I prayed, "God of justice . . . fix this and free your child."

When I got back to the car, I drove to a diner and read as much as I could about the case. The evidence is out there and easily available. After a few hours, I began driving home. Throughout the journey, I grew angrier and angrier that the State of Tennessee was so dedicated to killing Andrew Thomas. Somewhere around Memphis, I pulled over and got out of my car. At the top of my lungs, I screamed out into the bitter freezing night air, "Andrew Thomas is innocent!" While I doubt many people heard me, it was then that I decide to not stop screaming until they do.

Amen.

JANUARY 3, 2016

Sheikh Nimr al-Nimr Lives! : A Word to Christians

Throughout the last five years, I've followed the case of human rights champion Saudi Arabian Shia Sheikh Nimr al-Nimr. With tacit affirmation from the United States, the Saudi government has brutally repressed all dissent. Coming from an oppressed religious minority, Sheikh Nimr sought to bring about a better world for his fellow Shias in Saudi Arabia through nonviolent resistance. Instead of listening to him, the Saudis executed him earlier today. If you want to know what Ghandi or Dr. King looks like today, look no further than Sheikh Nimr. Throughout the world, churches should be in deep mourning over the lose of this great prophet. Unfortunately, most Christians can't imagine Jesus wearing a turban. I can. I want to be just like him. Despite the sting of death, I praise Allah that Sheikh Nimr al-Nimr lives!

Amen.

JANUARY 6, 2016

The Sad Case of Dr. Larycia Hawkins

Do Muslims and Christians worship the same God? Dr. Larycia Hawkins believes so. Wheaton College is determined to fire her for such beliefs. Ever since Dr. Hawkins wore a hijab during Advent in solidarity with Muslims, I've watched this story unfold with mixed emotions. I agree with Dr. Hawkins on Muslims. I find many of my Muslim friends to be more like Jesus than most Christians I know. I don't want Dr. Hawkins to be fired. I believe she is a brave woman that can do much good at a place like Wheaton. However, it is important to point out the deeply problematic nature of working at Wheaton in the first place. The statement of faith that Dr. Hawkins signed and reaffirmed just last month is textbook conservative evangelicalism and filled with beliefs that have proven incredibly harmful to a wide variety of people. From the historical personhood of Adam and Eve to ideas of substitutionary atonement to a literal hell to the impending return of Jesus, Dr. Hawkins believes some really problematic doctrines. Let's also not forget that Wheaton has treated LGBT staff and students horribly during Dr. Hawkins tenure and she obviously held on to her job in the midst of those injustices. While I think it's important to push for her to keep her job, I think we all need to be careful before we act like Dr. Hawkins is a beacon of progressive thought. She's not.

Amen.

JANUARY 8, 2016

Repent! Follow Jesus! : A Plea for Radicalism

Originally appeared in Baptist News Global on 1/8/2016

"With every head bowed and every eye closed . . . " I peeked. "Who would like to ask Jesus to be their personal savior and start walking with him tonight? Raise your hand and live forever!" I used one eye to scan the room. The craziest lady in the room was waving her hand back and forth. "Will all who raised your hand join us at the front of the sanctuary?" I was nervous for her. After a few people went down, the crazy lady stood up and started shrieking in jubilation. Every butt in the room squeezed so tight that I just knew that all the pew cushions would be gone when they stood up. People didn't know what was going to happen next. The crazy lady just kept dancing her way down the aisle. In modern discourse, I actually think I'd call it holy twerking. When she finally arrived down front, everyone just wanted it to stop. This was an orderly people. They didn't want all this foolishness in church. The pastor insinuated that the crazy lady had some intellectual struggles. When someone asked whether she had the capacity to make a decision to follow Jesus, the pastor didn't miss a beat, "She has more sense than all of you. For in the last few minutes, she showed us that following Jesus takes place despite the institutional church not because of it. I encourage you to learn from her enthusiasm." The woman didn't seem so crazy anymore. After she was unanimously received into the fellowship, the pastor asked if she would like to say anything to her new community. In a strong piercing voice, the lady said, "Follow Jesus!"

Follow Jesus? Order is our God. We've decided that following Jesus doesn't fit with our institutional sensibilities. We would rather sit easily under our stained glass than have difficult conversations about racism. Keeping our music going is so much more important than having conversations about homophobia and transphobia. We take up collections and pray for the poor without ever talking about how we are doing very little to be in solidarity with the poor. Everybody wants to celebrate women a few days each year but nobody wants to work to discuss transforming our sexist society. Over and over again on the most important issues of our day, we simply don't care about going further than a few words and some false empathy. If our services go well, we see a little growth and we keep the lights on, nothing else matters. We want nothing to do with Jesus. We want to survive. Order is our God.

Fanny Crosby can help us with a theme song for our age:

Pass us now, O demanding Savior,
Don't trouble us with any of their cries;
We are just trying to keep the lights on,
Please just pass us by.

Welcome to Christianity without Jesus . . . where we spend all of our time on issues that love settled long ago.

"We need these guns to protect us." I couldn't believe that one of the larger progressive churches in the South had armed guards. I couldn't hold back. "Jesus doesn't attend any church with guns." Guns are the exact opposite of Jesus. Guns kill. Jesus gives life. Owning or carrying a gun is tantamount to turning your back on Jesus. Why would any church have to struggle with whether to allow guns in their churches?

The Violence of Being

"There are few more violent of acts perpetuated against Christians of color than our consistent depictions of a white Jesus." Speaking at a progressive church, I felt I had to say something about the white stained glass Jesus over my head. Friends, Jesus was never white. These depictions are racist. *What* would make us delay in removing depictions of a white Jesus?

"Jesus would have us protect our borders." I was appalled when I heard First Baptist Dallas Pastor Dr. Robert Jeffress utter these words. Unfortunately, people in most of *our* churches live like they're true. Can you imagine Jesus living comfortably behind the borders of the richest nation on the planet? We can't follow Jesus without getting uncomfortable. Have you opened your church to housing immigrants yet?

"We are going slow on the LGBT issue." It's 2015. If you don't celebrate LGBT people in your church, you don't have Jesus. There is no more conversation to be had. There is only Jesus. Why do you continue to exclude those Jesus loves?

The music is playing. The pastor is begging. The aisle is open. Put down the order. Put down the budget. Put down the guns. Put down the white Jesus. Put down the borders. Put down the exclusion. Put down all that makes you comfortable. Put down Christianity without Jesus. Don't tarry. Don't delay. Feel the pull of radicalism. This is the hour. This is the moment. Repent! Follow Jesus!

Amen.

JANUARY 10, 2016

The God in the Table

*Preached at The Church at the Table in Denton, Texas on 1/10/16

A LIGHT IN THE ATTIC
Shel Silverstein

There's a light in the attic.
Thought the house is dark and shuttered,
I can see a flickerin' flutter,
And I know what it's about.
There's a light on in the attic.
I can see it from the outside,
And I know you're on the inside . . . lookin' out.

When I started thinking about meeting all of you in the intimacy of this space, I wanted to bring a word that would help you live into a spirituality that is beyond church. I have come to believe that only when we dare to go beyond church do we actually become the church. For the church as it is expressed in our modern culture is a cheap imitation of what is to come. I was praying we might touch some of what is to come tonight.

Emily has helped me to ponder our relationship to things. There is a light in the attic. Does whatever creates that light matter? I believe so. I believe the light in things matters more than we could ever imagine. The light draws us to ponder things. The light connects to things. The light is in this table we sit around tonight.

Jesus gathers the disciples around the table for the last meal. If we rush to the serving of the body and blood, we will miss something very important . . . the table that has pulled them together. There is a light within the table that gives light. There is a light within the table that calls light out. May it be so tonight.

Things matter.

The God in the table draws us. We gather around this table to experience God. There is something immaterial going on in this table. Whatever draws us to love has God in it.

The God in the table creates intimacy. We want to share with each other tonight for no other reason than intimacy is created when we sit around this table.

The God in the table pushes us out. We find love around the table in then we leave the table to take love to others. The love that the table shares changes us so that we might change the world.

Let us give thanks for the love in this table. Let us give thanks for the God in this table.

May the things we have found make us a light to all we meet.

Amen.

JANUARY 11, 2016

Barbara Dawson: A Child of God Slaughtered by Medical Capitalism and Our Police State

"I can't breathe." The cry has gone out over and over again. On December 21, 2015, the cry was heard again.

After complaining of stomach pain, Barbara Dawson was rushed to Calhoun Liberty Hospital in Blountstown, Florida. Upon stabilization, the medical staff demanded Dawson leave the premises. Repeatedly, Dawson expressed that she didn't feel well and begged to stay. The staff then banned her from the hospital and called police. When the Blountstown police officer came into the room, Dawson screamed, "No! No! No!" Despite pleading for further help, Dawson was forced out of the hospital. Throughout the ordeal, Dawson screamed out, "Oh my God, oh my God, oh my God." Right before the officer tried to force her in the cruiser, Dawson collapsed. The officer thought she was faking and proceeded to threaten her. By the time a doctor finally came out, Dawson was dying. A short time later, Barbara Dawson was dead.

Jesus encountered many Pharisees in his life. Over and over, the Pharisees destroyed lives based on their greed and prejudice. On multiple occasions, Jesus pushed back and in our modern lingo probably declared, "Fuck the Pharisees!"

Barbara Dawson encountered multiple Pharisees on the last night of her life. There was the medical staff and hospital administration at Calhoun Liberty Hospital who slung her into the dirt and left her to die because she was costing the institution too much money. There was the Blountstown police officer that thought an overweight black woman was wasting his time. I believe that Jesus would stand with those who dare resist the evils of medical capitalism and our police state and loudly declare, "Fuck Calhoun Liberty Hospital! Fuck the Blountstown Police!"

Stop killing black people!
Stop killing the disabled!
Stop killing the poor!
Stop killing the marginalized!
Stop killing!

Amen.

http://www.cnn.com/2016/01/07/us/florida-woman-removed-hospital-dies/

JANUARY 13, 2016

Dallas Celebrates the White Dr. Martin Luther, King, Jr.

Growing up in Atlanta, I was well aware from an early age that the celebration of Dr. Martin Luther King, Jr. was serious business. On numerous occasions, I traveled to Ebenezer Baptist Church to participate in the annual commemoration services. A few years back, I will never forget Dr. Cornel West warning us about those leading the "Santa-Clausification" of Dr. King by sanitizing his radical prophetic message. When I saw the advertisements for Dallas' Annual Dr. Martin Luther King, Jr. Parade & Celebration, I was shocked. Here in Dallas, not only has the political and corporate establishment succeeded in recently taking over the parade, they have actually made Dr. King white in their advertisements. No wonder we can't get any action on police brutality in this city.

Amen.

JANUARY 16, 2016

True Pastors Don't Endorse Candidates!

Back in October, I was absolutely appalled at the spectacle of seeing a room full of evangelical pastors fawning all over Donald Trump. Not long after the circus, the Pastor of First Baptist Dallas Dr. Robert Jeffress stood in front of another circus to pray for and practically endorse Trump at one of his rallies. On the other side, pastors are also rushing out to endorse and champion Hillary Clinton and Bernie Sanders. To make matters worse, pastors also seem to think that they need to make state and local endorsements. Over and over, I continue to watch pastors sell off their potential prophetic voices to the highest bidder. I don't remember Jesus ever endorsing any candidates. I think he was smart enough to know that an endorsement limits your ability to speak prophetically to whoever is elected and limits you ability to minister to the whole populace after the election.

In 2008, I got excited about Barack Obama. I bought the shirt, hat and bumper sticker. I was two years past my ordination as pastor. Early one Saturday morning, I'll never forget sitting down with a cherished mentor. As I proudly wore my Obama shirt, my mentor leaned in and said, "How are you going to demand that the Obama not bomb some poor nation after you have run around with his shirt on? How are you going to minister to those who hate Obama after they see you with that shirt on? True pastors don't endorse candidates!" I believed her then. After seeing President

True Pastors Don't Endorse Candidates!

Obama violate my Christian faith by bombing countless nations and watching our nation become as polarized as I've ever seen it, I believe her more now.

Amen.

JANUARY 18, 2016

The Thingyness of God

*Based on a talk delivered at The Church of the Table in Fort Worth on 1/17/2016

The great woods were magnificent. Though I'd hiked many places, I'd never experienced anything like this. There was energy to the place that was unexplainable. The things that surrounded me were so full of God. The trees swayed their joy. The wind whispered love. The leaves crunched a welcome. The sun embraced me. I hope to go back there some day. If I never do, I will know that it was there that I learned about the energy of God in things.

The thingyness of things has always caused us to assume that things are meaningless. If God created all things, then the energy that unites all things is holy. When Jesus gathered disciples for one last supper, do you not think there was powerful energy in everything in that place? Was there not energy flowing into and out of the table? Was there not energy in the cup from which they all drank? Will there not be energy in the bread and wine that we will consume for communion? Things contain energy that points beyond the thing just like we do. Things have the energy of the creator within them. When we commune with things we are communing with the very essence of God . . . energy. Make no mistake, the energy of God flows through all that is and all that will ever be. The thingyness of God can never be denied.

The Thingyness of God

This evening, we all came together seeking something more. We gathered around a thing . . . this table . . . with divine expectations. There is a thingyness about our gathering. On some level, it was energy that pulled us together around a thing seeking the thingyness of God. Perhaps, the thingyness of God will be what sustains us until we meet again.

Amen.

JANUARY 19, 2016

Release the Names! : An Address to the Dallas County Commissioners Court

Today, I'm here to speak on behalf of the Joseph Hutcheson family. On August 1, 2015 around 10am, Hutcheson parked his truck on the curb outside the Lew Sterrett Justice Center here in Dallas County and hysterically ran up the hill. Upon entering the lobby, Hutcheson loudly proclaimed, "Please don't hurt me, I just need some help." According to the Dallas Morning News and now a videotape of the incident, deputies from the Dallas County Sheriff's Department ultimately pounced on Hutcheson. One placed a knee to Hutcheson's back. One placed a knee to Hutcheson's neck that turned into a knee to the throat. The last time I spoke to you all, we only knew about those things from eyewitness accounts. Now, we have videotape of the incident. These pieces of information are fact. After Hutcheson went unconscious, there was an extended period of time that he didn't receive proper medical attention. So whether the Dallas County Sheriff's Department is guilty of killing Hutcheson through physical violence or neglect to render medical aid quickly, what we know from what the Dallas County Medical Examiner has already told us what is . . . this was and is a homicide that the Sheriff's Department is responsible for. In a typical homicide the family gets to know who the authorities believe is responsible for the death. In a typical homicide the family gets to know who the suspect or suspects might be. In this case, we are going on six months since this happened and we have no idea who these deputies were. The citizens of Dallas County deserve to know who they are encountering when they enter the lobby of their jail. Right now, we have no idea who is in that lobby. I wouldn't want my wife or children or anyone I love or for that matter anyone to get a pat down from one of the deputies who killed Joseph Hutcheson. They might end up with a knee in their throat. How is the public supposed to hold deputies accountable for repeated acts of police brutality when we're not told the names of those who commit such acts? I respectfully ask for your help.

Amen.

JANUARY 20, 2016

I Believe in IT : The God Beyond God

While language can only take us so far . . . there are times in which our current language is not taking us far enough and other words can take us further. Tonight, I want us to explore that it would look like to shift our language concerning God. I believe that the word "it" points further into the distance of possibility and imagination than the word "God" is capable. Certainly time manipulates language and our time is one in which God language has lost a tremendous amount of positive meaning. I know that the word "God" is very hurtful to many of you. For me, "IT" is able to describe the unlimited indescribable possibilities of divinity in a way that "God" cannot. The question of our hour thus shifts from "What is God?" to "What is IT?" Come let us dream . . .

In the beginning was IT. IT was with God. IT was God. What is IT? IT is mystery beyond. IT is magic beyond magic. IT is imagination beyond imagination. IT is love beyond love. IT is divinity beyond divinity. What is IT? IT is. The isity of IT is the divinity of IT. In the is of IT is the was, the is and the eternal will be. I believe in IT because there is an is that has been with me. IT found me. IT called me. IT pushes me. IT is with me. IT found is tonight. IT calls us. IT pushes us. IT is with us. IT is.

How often have you asked the question: "What is it?" Is this not a divine question? By asking the name of it are we not recognizing the divinity of IT? Do we not believe in an IT that is everywhere and in everything? IT is here. IT is there. IT is everywhere. One of great tragedies of Christianity is the murder of divinity everywhere. Through systemization and institutionalization, IT was murdered somewhere along the way. While the concept died . . . IT lives.

Churches can't contain IT. That's why we're not there. IT is here.

Amen.

JANUARY 20, 2016

The Case of Richard Masterson

While I've never published this type of damning report about someone who is about to be executed before, I think this case calls for it. I believe that Richard Masterson is beyond mentally incompetent. I can think of few things more cruel or unusual than to execute someone who is out of their mind. Tonight, the State of Texas will try to do just that. I will be standing outside the Huntsville Unit in protest. Below, are my memories of my last visit with Masterson in October that I recorded and submitted to try to help save his life in his appeals process.

Memories of a Visit with Richard Masterson

On October 15, 2015, I walked to a booth about halfway down the middle row in the visitation room at the Polunsky Unit and sat. For a few minutes, I waited in prayer. I opened my eyes when I heard the door clank. Looking up, my eyes beheld a man who looked out of his mind. From his wildly dilated pupils to the strange contortions of his face, I knew something wasn't right. When I picked up the phone, Richard Masterson began to rage. I've never had that level of anger directed at me before. Over and over, Masterson told me, "I'm not gay!" I didn't care. I still don't understand why he felt the need to keep telling me that. For almost two hours, I felt the conversation grow crazier and crazier. It took all the spiritual energy I had not to get up and leave.

The Case of Richard Masterson

Masterson repeatedly told me that he wanted to die. Then, he switched gears rapidly and told me that he had a girlfriend that made him want to live. The more Masterson talked, the more confused I got. Statement after statement seemed to contradict the last. When I asked if he liked any of the guards or anyone he was housed with, Masterson told me that he wished he could kill a few of them "with his bare hands." He also pointed to the outside to assure me that there were people out there he would like to kill too. When I asked him why he would say such things when he knew he was being recorded, he shrugged and replied that he didn't give a shit.

When I told Masterson that I was a minister, he proceeded to tell me about his attraction to Transgender women. Repeatedly, Masterson told me, "There ain't no pussy like a brand new pussy." I heard more stories than I ever wanted to hear in my life about "new pussies." Then, Masterson assured me again that he wasn't gay. When I asked about the Transgender woman he was convicted of strangling to death, Masterson got really belligerent and told me, "I ain't scared to strangle nobody." Then, he told me again that he wasn't gay. If he said that he wasn't gay once, I bet he said it at least ten or eleven times. Though I managed to take a picture with Masterson, he acted paranoid about that as well. From the words that he said to the way that his body looked, Richard Masterson repeatedly proved to me that he was out of his mind.

Throughout the conversation, Masterson kept exhibiting a mix of rage and psychosis. The words that did make sense were strangely combative. The rest I found nuts. As someone who has ministered to numerous people struggling with all types of mental conditions, I have no question that Richard Masterson is not in his right mind and probably never was. Judging from my visit, I believe it would be cruel and unusual to execute Masterson.

Amen.

JANUARY 21, 2016

The Incarnation of Jesus . . . Anthony Hill

In Matthew 25:40, Jesus said, "What you have done to the least of these, you have done to me." Last year in a metropolitan suburb of Atlanta, Georgia, a young unarmed and naked mentally ill veteran by the name of Anthony Hill was running around his apartment complex. Concerned residents called police and Dekalb County Officer Robert Olsen responded to the scene. When Hill trotted towards him, Olsen shot and killed Hill. In those moments, Hill was the least and most vulnerable amongst us. Jesus has declared that he becomes the least and most vulnerable amongst us. In those moments, Anthony Hill became the incarnation of Jesus. If we want to live in a more just and compassionate society, we would do well to look to the incarnation of Jesus in Hill and learn to prevent what happened to him from ever happening again. While I am pleased that Officer Robert Olsen was indicted earlier today for Hill's murder, I will not stop praying with my feet until we get these murderous cops off the street.

Amen.

JANUARY 25, 2016

Presence is the Antidote to Killing

Originally Appeared in Waging NonViolence.

Last Wednesday, I took a short walk from my car to stand on the corner outside the old red prison walls of the Huntsville Unit in Huntsville as Texas killed Richard Masterson. Having led the nation for many decades, executions are a fairly routine event for Texans. Only the most ardent abolitionists show up to voice opposition. In those difficult hours as the sun started to set, I joined about a dozen others standing in defiance. .While there was really nothing I could do, I've never grown comfortable just standing there. The closer the moment gets the more restless I always become. I thought about charging the building. I knew that was just a fantasy. I was stuck. I started to pray. I couldn't even understand my own prayers. I knew I couldn't stop them. What good was I to Masterson now? Seeing me physically struggling, an old friend leaned over and said, "Your presence is enough." The words of an old nun I heard long ago ruminated in my ears, "Presence is the antidote to killing."

I don't believe in killing people. When I was a child, I learned about God killing a bunch of people in a flood. Before I could give it a second thought, I decided I didn't believe in that right then and there. God doesn't kill people. We do. Over the years, I've clung to Jesus for guidance in the midst of the killing. While loving your neighbor as yourself has never been vogue, I've tried to spread the message as best as I can. Repeatedly in the midst of crisis, I've had to remind people that loving and killing don't go together. There is no way to lovingly kill your neighbor. I figured that this was an exceedingly logical conclusion. Then, I moved to Texas.

While killing is terrible, it's even worse to be around it and not do anything about it. When I moved here almost four years ago, I knew had to do something about the constant executions Texas was carrying out. Unfortunately, I didn't know how to make a difference. From the shower to the car to the church to everywhere I went, I couldn't think of anything else. Then, the Spirit of God snuck up on me. At an interfaith breakfast in Dallas almost three years ago, a Buddhist monk named Tashi Nyima stood up and relayed a story about giving our bodies to conversations for justice. I knew what I needed to do. I needed to start walking. Since then, I've trekked and hosted events on a small group 35-mile journey from Dallas (high death sentencing area) to Fort Worth (high death sentencing area), a solo 200-mile journey from Livingston (home of death row) to Austin (state capitol) and a solo 43-mile journey from Livingston to Huntsville (execution chamber). Just last year, I even got invited to help lead a couple of dozen walkers on an 80-mile journey for abolition in Ohio from Lucasville (death row) to Columbus (execution chamber).

In moment after moment along the way, people have joined me and discovered their passion for abolition. Here in Texas, we have seen a steady increase in participation in abolition groups and a decline in new death sentences. Though the work is slow, I believe the death penalty is on the way out. I'm praying for a ruling from the United States Supreme Court that the death penalty is unconstitutionally cruel and unusual punishment. Until then, I just try to be present. Truthfully, all of my journeys have led to moments where I wondered if I was doing anything productive. In those hours of struggle, the words of the old nun always come back, "Presence is the antidote to killing."
Amen.

JANUARY 25, 2016

What Does God Look Like?

*The Church at the Table in Oak Lawn on 1/25/2016.

The looks of God are a curious thing to explore. However, I also think such attributes are something we can't ignore. We are made in God's image. What does God look like? God looks like us. We look like God. If you want to know what God looks like, look around. The God in whose image we are made looks like us. God is many colors, shapes, sizes, abilities and other looks and ways of being. God is all of it.

Most would assume that God doesn't look like anything that we assume is undesirable. Why is it so far outside of our consideration to think of God having Down's syndrome? I believe it is because we assume that God is perfect and that there is something imperfect about Down's syndrome. I can think of nothing more evil that to assume that someone doesn't carry the image of God. We are made in God's image. God reflects us all and all means all.

Many would say that God looks like Jesus. Throughout the county in church after church, you run into these white Jesuses made of stained glass. Obviously, there is a belief amongst many that Jesus reflects our dominate culture. The dominant culture always assumes that they own God or Jesus and God or Jesus looks like them. This is evil of the highest order. Disordered thinking such as this corrupts not only the image of God but also the image that

The Violence of Being

we have of ourselves. There is no question that the way that we perceive God is tied to the way that we perceive ourselves. Our identity-based culture is causing us to lose connection with ourselves. We are all made in the image of God. We are enough in our very person. We don't need the dominant culture to affirm that. We just have to look for the God within. We jsut need to look for God.

For over 50 years, we have seen the release of identity theologies. These theologies have helped us to recapture our image in the image of God. God is black. God is brown. God is female. God is disabled. The theologies run the spectrum of identities. The problem with such theologies is that they often take us to the oppression olympics where we find people fighting about God being here and not there or there and not here. We cannot separate God from ourselves. When we separate ourselves from the image of God by categorization and identification we become broken people. God is beyond our lines. God is as colorful or diverse as can ever be imagined or dreamed. We can't be in right relationship with each other as long as we are holding the lines. The ists, isms and phobia are a product of a broken relationship with God and self. We must get saved from our ordered disordered thinking.

God is mentally ill. God has AIDS. God has cancer. God is everything and anything that we are. God looks like us. We follow the sick crazy colorful God. We are made in God's image. God exists in our image. God looks like us.

Amen.

JANUARY 26, 2016

Jesus: "Fuck the Police"

While on routine patrol of Brooklyn, New York's Pink Houses with his gun drawn and finger on the trigger (something law enforcement are trained to never do), rookie officer Peter Liang was startled by Akai Gurley and fired. The bullet tore through Gurley's heart and the innocent man bled out as Liang tried to figure out how to keep his job in the midst of this major accident. Despite being trained in CPR, Liang did nothing to try to save Gurley's life. Neighbors called for help. Despite more officers arriving, Gurley's girlfriend was the only person who attempted CPR. Currently, Liang is on trial facing charges of manslaughter and criminally negligent homicide. From report after report, we know this is not an isolated incident. If Jesus spoke at this trial or any other where the police were actually being held accountable for their actions, I know exactly how he'd begin . . .

"You brood of vipers! How can you speak good things, when you are evil?"

In Matthew 12:34, Jesus condemned another group that brutalized and terrorized the people called the Pharisees. In a few sentences, Jesus let there be no mistake whose side he was on. In the midst of the brutality and terrorism of our police, I don't question whose side Jesus is on.

Close to thirty years ago, rap supergroup NWA gave us words to deal with such a time as this. I believe Jesus would use them . . .

The Violence of Being

"Fuck tha Police"

Amen.

JANUARY 26, 2016

Tonight, We Were Dining with God.

Emily and I don't have much money. Truthfully, the vegetables and rice were the best we could do tonight. We were tired. It didn't matter. The kids were hungry. The words "money" and "tired" are not a part of their vocabulary. By the time everyone got to their plate, we were even more exhausted. In the midst of the chaos, we just wanted everyone to eat and go to bed. Then, something magical happened.

I looked up and the symphony commenced. Emulating the creator of us all, Phillip playfully created bubbles in his drink. Just like the divine whispers that often sneak up on us, Jeff told us that he loves us. Much like the many languages of the divine, Quinley kept pulling new words out of his head. In his silence, Lucas reminded us of God's silence. In her desire to get out of her chair, Madeleine reminded us that God can't be restrained. Ultimately, the scales fell from our eyes and the realization hit.

Tonight, we were dining with God.

Amen.

JANUARY 29, 2016

The Crime Was Horrible

*Originally appeared in the Denton Record Chronicle

To the Editor:

The crime was horrendous. By all accounts, Marion and Linda Scott were beautiful loving people. Even if they weren't, there was no reason for the evil that took place. For slashing his parents until they had no breath, Stephen Scott deserves to die. But, who deserves to kill him? I remember Jesus saying that whoever is without sin can cast the first lethal injection, or something like that. If we kill Scott, we deserve the same punishment he does. Killing is killing. What is more, the Dallas Morning News estimates that it is three times more expensive to carry out the death penalty than it is to put someone in prison for the rest of their natural lives. How Christian would it be to sacrifice public services in order to kill Scott? I would imagine cuts in mental health services would lead to more tragedies just like the one Scott set in motion. Which reminds me, how could we ever even consider killing someone who was suffering from the mental health struggles that Scott has? Honestly, I can't believe a county full of Christians would even consider such a thing. I guess we're Christians except when it comes to killing and mental health. I pray I'm wrong. The death penalty isn't about Scott . . . it's about us.

Rev. Dr. Jeff Hood
Board of Directors, Texas Coalition to Abolish Death Penalty
Denton, Texas

JANUARY 31, 2016

The Shirt

words of comfort for a grieving friend.

I laid it out.
I waited for the time.
I heard you call.
I said goodbye.

I went to the shirt.
I held it tight.
I knew the time was finally right.

I put it on.
I drove to church.
I got up to speak.
It was here that I knew we'd meet.

I wore the shirt.

FEBRUARY 3, 2016

Government Should be Afraid of Christians / A Word from Zimbabwe

"He's the best leader in the world." On my final flight into Zimbabwe, I overheard a gentleman make this comment about President Robert Mugabe. When I asked about all the crippling economic struggles the nation was having (unemployment at 90% and multiple government sectors having gone unpaid for 6 months), he looked at me and said, "Christians should fear the President. This is the only path to peace." Shocked, I let the conversation drift off.

Peace is an illusion when people are starving to death. Christians have a pivotal prophetic role to play in the midst of such glaring injustice. We can either be on the side of sustenance or starvation. You can't follow Jesus and cling to a false peace. We were warned about those who would declare peace when there is no peace. As famine approaches in Zimbabwe (nearly a quarter of Zimbabwe's population are at risk of death), I hope to encourage all that I meet to use their faith to fight for the food they need to survive. In the midst of stunning economic inequalities (President Mugabe rolling around in a new Mercedes and asking the government to pay for lavish parties), Jesus is for eating more than Jesus is for a false peace. As for the fear piece, government should be afraid of Christians far more than Christians should be afraid of government.

Amen.

FEBRUARY 4, 2016

The Mentally Ill of Zimbabwe

After three days traveling, I was not in the best mental health. Between the mania and depression, I was struggling to figure out how to make it the rest of the trip. Then, a phrase gave me more clarity about where I was.

"Don't tell anyone you're mentally ill." There are few phrases that can strike more fear in someone whose brain functions differently than others. After hearing the phrase, I decided I needed to learn even more and do something.

People of faith in Zimbabwe have long declared that mental illness is a result of the demonic. When someone is struggling to keep control of their mind, they're often restrained and/or beaten until the demon comes out. When the restraint and/or beating doesn't work, people are sometimes killed. When I asked a nurse how often this happens, she said, "Regularly." Even in death the mentally ill are stigmatized and shamed. The mentally ill dead not allowed to be buried with their family and it's assumed that one can still get the demon once they're in the ground. When I inquired why more money isn't spent to educate people, another healthcare told me, "Mental illness is not profitable in this country." No matter where I go, money seems to drive morals. Another teacher told me, "Let me assure you, in Zimbabwe it is more dangerous to be mentally ill than it is to be gay." Due to the lack of information in the United States about the struggles of the mentally ill in Zimbabwe, I had no idea. Due to the struggle to secure widespread information, it is difficult to speak to the number of people killed. With as much as 10% of the population suffering from some form of serious mental illness, the healthcare professionals I spoke with estimated that thousands are killed each year.

When I thought about how Jesus would respond to such oppression and marginalization, I didn't have to think long about what my sermon is going to be on Sunday:

The Mentally Ill God.

Amen.

FEBRUARY 5, 2016

The Chickens

Birds of a feather flock together. Strangely, I've found companions amongst the feathers on the farm. There is just something about these chickens.

Back feathers. White feathers. Brown feathers. Green feathers. Their brilliant colors seem to never end. The feathered rainbow calls me to never stop searching for more colors.

Noise catches their attention. Immediately, the chickens run as fast as they can. It is as if the whole world will crash if they don't get there first. The feathered sprinters call me to run and not grow weary.

Necks of beautiful color arise and feathers extend. When you see this, you know that someone has been pecking around too much. I saw many feathers fly today. The feathered peckers remind me to keep a stiff neck in a world of injustice.

Flight comes from the full extension of wings that are not made to carry the bird too far. It doesn't matter. The chickens repeatedly kept going for it. In the midst of a world trying to keep you grounded, the feathered flyers encouraged me to keep extending my wings.

Chicken toenails are fierce. The brilliantly colored legs look like they are ready to survive whatever the world brings. While neither are all that attractive, they combine to help the bird take on the shit. The feathered trailblazers pushed me to dig deep and push through.

When I picked one of the birds up, I felt the presence of the divine. God made these birds to be words of life to us all. I'm not too chicken to listen.

Amen.

FEBRUARY 6, 2016

The Impromptu Sermon : Thoughts of Christian Defiance in Zimbabwe

Earlier this afternoon, a group of Zimbabwean government officials asked me to discuss politics with them. This is an authoritarian society where such an invitation can be dangerous. Nevertheless, I engaged. When I told them that I was primarily a theologian, they told me that here in Zimbabwe politics and spirituality don't mix. While I didn't know if such a comment was intended to be a warning or not, I questioned them as to whether Christianity could even exist in such a space. When they inquired what I meant, I began.

Throughout the Gospels, Jesus commits acts of political revolution. Repeatedly, Jesus refused to be bound by laws that sought to segregate and divide the population. In direct defiance of the government, Jesus kept breaking the law to be with the people. The lines that the government of Zimbabwe has drawn would not be able to hold Jesus back. When a woman that was caught in adultery was about to be executed, Jesus placed his body between the executioners and the woman. Can you imagine if Christians in Zimbabwe started to place their bodies between all of the people who are disappeared and killed? Jesus was a revolutionary. When Jesus saw the government cheating people out of their money like the police bribe people in this country, Jesus overturned their tables and tossed them out. Jesus was so much more than just a spiritual leader. In Matthew 25, Jesus declared that he would place his very person with the marginalized and oppressed. In Zimbabwe, this means that Jesus would stand with the political revolutionaries seeking a better world, the hungry, those who are not being paid by the government, the mentally ill and a whole host of others who are mistreated and sometimes killed by the actions of this government. Make no mistake, Jesus was a political revolutionary and paid the price for it. Ultimately, political forces executed Jesus. Make no mistake, Robert Mugabe would kill Jesus and intends to kill anyone who follows his way of revolution. With Jesus, there was and is no separating politics and spirituality.

When I finished talking, no one spoke. I don't think they'd heard the Gospel presented like this before. Before hundreds of thousands more people die due to the tanking economy and the approaching famine, I pray that God will remove Robert Mugabe from his luxurious accommodations and his position as President. I hope that Christians will follow Jesus and be helpful in this process.

Amen.

FEBRUARY 7, 2016

The Mentally Ill God: A Sermon from Zimbabwe

*Delivered at Monomotapa Baptist Church in Gweru, Zimbabwe on 2/7/2016

Throughout Zimbabwe, I've heard something repeatedly . . . that social and political realities have nothing to do with spiritual realities. In the United States, people say similar things when they don't want you to talk about things. People want to keep God way up in the clouds. For if God is up there, then those in power don't have to worry about struggling with the God down here. When you leave God out of our social and political realities, you leave Jesus out of God. For when God came to earth, God was constantly involved in social and political issues. Think about God engaging public health. Think about the racial and economic lines that God repeatedly crossed. Think about God tossing out the public officials outside the Temple. Through Jesus, God engaged in social and political realities all the time. To say otherwise, is to deny the Gospel.

When people are starving . . . when people have nothing . . . when the helpless are trampled . . . when corruption has taken over . . . when people are living under a government that does not care if they live or die . . . God is there . . . Jesus is there. I've been thinking about the way that the mentally ill are treated around the world. I've been told that in extreme efforts to heal or contain . . . the mentally ill are sometimes injured or even killed. People of faith in the United States do similar things. They don't understand the physiological realities of someone who is mentally ill. I would imagine the same is true here. Some might question talking about mental illness in church. If we are to follow the Gospel, we are intrinsically connected to the least of these amongst us. Jesus said, "What you have done to the least of these you have done to me." God said, "What you have done to the least of these you have done to me." The mentally ill are the least of the least. God is mentally ill.

Can you imagine God sitting in darkness before creation? The mental illness keeps growing and growing. Eventually, God creates light to try to get some relief. That didn't work. God creates water to try to get some relief. That didn't work. God creates animals. That didn't work. If there was to be any relief of the mental illness, God realized that God had to create something to love in God's image. When the medicine arrived, God took a long time to get accustomed to it. Throughout the Old Testament, one can see that God is struggling. From the Flood to a couple of Genocides, God couldn't get control and kept hurting people. The incarnation of God in Jesus was a shock therapy. Can you imagine the shock of the smell of shit in Bethlehem? God shocked us and we shocked God. We ultimately shocked God to death. Love was the medicine that brought God back. Though slightly better, God remains mentally ill.

We must stand with God. We must stand with the least of these. We must stand with the mentally ill. We must rebel against the government when the government is not helping. We must take the place of the government when the government is not helping. We must be the hands and feet of God to the mentally ill no matter what it takes. May this church be a leader of reform efforts in the treatment of the mentally ill. It is time for Christians everywhere to stand with the mentally ill.

THE MENTALLY ILL GOD: A SERMON FROM ZIMBABWE

Let us remember that Jesus said . . . God said . . . "I was mentally ill and you either visited me or you didn't." Will you embrace the mentally ill? Will you embrace the Mentally Ill God?

Before we go, I have one more thing to share with you, "I am mentally ill."

Amen.

FEBRUARY 7, 2016

Baptist Colors in Zimbabwe

Baptists are a factional bunch. We part ways when we can't agree on the way the chairs are arranged. Things get interesting when Baptists decide to stay together. Throughout my upbringing, I watched conflicted Baptist churches affiliate with multiple denominations to appease everyone. I remember some churches were aligned with as many as eight different denominations at one time. Though I didn't expect it to be different in Zimbabwe, there was something unique that caught my eye.

Within the church I was at this morning, there were women affiliated with two different Baptist denominational bodies. One group wore blue and gold with their denominational logos affixed to their clothing and the other group wore purple with their denominational logos affixed to their clothing. Though I didn't see it at the church, I saw men in similar outfits representing their denominations later in the day. Regardless, I started thinking about what it would be like if Baptists in the United States did this. Baptists would certainly have colorful congregations.

Wouldn't it be nice to see everyone's true colors?

Amen.

FEBRUARY 8, 2016

Resisting Mugabe in Zimbabwe

Dirt has been a constant companion. Like air, you're constantly breathing it in and exhaling it out. When the bus arrived, I passed through the red fog to the climb up into my seat. Before I could even think, the driver looked at me and said, "Why do you remain silent about what's going on here in Zimbabwe? We're living in hell. How many more people will have to disappear or starve to death before your people will care? Talking to you could get me killed." My stomach turned. There is no way to explain the silence of the world when it comes to Zimbabwe. When I mentioned that I was trying to write as much as I could, the driver shot back, "You must try harder. You are the only chance we have. Everyone here is terrified." I didn't ask many questions. Why should you when you already know the answers? After much listening, I managed one before I got out, "What does resistance look like here?" The driver didn't hesitate, "Prayer is my resistance. Every night when I go to sleep, I pray that I will wake up and Robert Mugabe will be dead."

While I was looking at newspapers on the street, the vendor looked up and inquired, "When are you going to help us with Mugabe?" Before I could respond, she slipped me an opposition paper and said, "This should help."

Later in the day, a local businessman approached me on the street. Unsure of what he was going to say, I let him do the talking.

"When I first learned about Hitler, I always wondered how people ever allowed a maniac to kill so many people. I don't wonder about that anymore. Now, I know. Here in Zimbabwe we are living it." After some further conversation, he looked me in the eye and said, "Please tell as many people as you can about our terror."

As I walked down the street, the Mercedes screeched to a stop. I wasn't far from the local offices of the intelligence service. "Are you that guy writing the articles and posting them on Facebook about the President?" The question hit me in the gut. After responding that I was, I answered his probing questions very carefully. At the first pause in the interaction, I began to walk away and heard, "Be careful during your time in Zimbabwe."

Many Zimbabweans have been fervent in their resistance for decades. The best that some can do are comments like the ones made to me throughout the day. After only a short period of time here, I've gotten a small taste of what happens to those who resist in this country. The difference is that I get to leave. When I do, I'll do all that I can to make the rest of the world aware of the evil of Mugabe and his followers in Zimbabwe. I pray you'll join me. Amen.

FEBRUARY 9, 2016

Where is Itai? : Thoughts on a Disappeared Man in Zimbabwe

On March 9, 2015, prominent Zimbabwean pro-democracy activist Itai Dzamara was abducted by what people believe to be government officials and has not been seen since. "Where is Itai?" The question is at the core of bubbling resistance.

On the 11th month since his disappearance, I decided to send a letter to the editors of the major opposition newspapers about Itai:

Editor-Just last week, I entered Zimbabwe for the first time. As a liberation theologian from the United States, I was hopeful to hear stories of people resisting the Mugabe regime. Instead, I've heard about chronic despair. The bus driver talked about being constantly afraid. The teacher talked about losing his farm. The businessman talked about corruption. The villagers talked about hunger. The student talked about leaving. The nurse talked about not getting paid. The clerk talked about pollution. The accounts of brutality were truly endless. I would imagine all the books of the world could not contain the present despair of Zimbabwe. People keep telling me that resistance is futile. Reading your news reminded me that Itai Dzamara didn't think so. Repeatedly, Itai risked his life seeking to liberate his country. Through his prophetic sacrifices, Itai is calling a people forward. Where is Itai? While I hope he's found alive, I pray that he will also be found alive in the hearts and minds of the people of this nation. Though I'll be leaving soon, I know he's in me.

Rev. Dr. Jeff Hood
Texas, USA

more info:

a link to an Amnesty International interview with Itai's wife: https://www.amnesty.org/en/latest/campaigns/2015/09/zimbabwe-where-is-itai-dzamara/

Pindula biography page:
http://www.pindula.co.zw/Itai_Dzamara

Amen.

FEBRUARY 10, 2016

The Ashes: A Celebration in Zimbabwe

The smells. The smoke. The bells. The masses.

The Roman Catholic Cathedral in Gweru, Zimbabwe is constructed to hold as many people as possible. Tonight, I watched thousands pour onto the small wooden benches. Then, the service began.

The words weren't different. Based on the structure of the service, I could've been in any Roman Catholic Church in the world. I wasn't.

People began to beat drums mightily. The masses started to glide down the aisle. The swaying. The claps. The movement. One by one, people returned from the altar with ashes ascribed to their foreheads. When it was my turn, I just started to move.

God was in the thumb that pressed the ashes against my forehead. God was in the ashes. God was in the lights. During those moments, God was everywhere.

By the time I returned to my seat, the entire congregation was standing in song. The words were familiar. "All to Jesus I surrender ... All to him I freely give ... " People were singing as loud as they could. I was too. Tears fell down my face. The power of Jesus to bring the world together was not lost on me. I was in it.

The Violence of Being

I didn't want it to end.

Maybe it won't.

Amen.

FEBRUARY 11, 2016

Zimbabwe Sleeping

The night brought fear
Peril filled my dreams
Would they come for us?
Who can say?

The dogs barked
My eyes shot open
Murmurs from my hosts
Was it our time?
Who can say?

We were followed
Are they here?
Who can say?

The happenings cycle
What was that noise?
What do they sound like?
Who can say?

The madness
Will it end?
Who can say?

FEBRUARY 12, 2016

Beauty: The Sunset Revelation

Sunsets are no respecters of our categories. The sun just sets and blazes her colors across the sky. Throughout my time in Zimbabwe, I've found beauty or perhaps beauty has found me. This evening is no different. As the sun slips past the clouds, I'm amazed at the people who stop. In the midst of the busy of the city, beauty still stops people right in their tracks. Looking deep into the heavens, they understand that they reflect the beauty of their creator. Straining with all my might, I climb higher and look harder to try to see too. For just a few moments, we all get it. Maybe it is the beauty that will save us.

Amen.

FEBRUARY 13, 2016

Lenten Remix 1: The Fluid John 3:16

"For God so loved the world that they gave their only them that whosoever believes in them shall not perish in the binaries but have fluidity everlasting."

For many years, I struggled with using plural pronouns as singular pronouns. Though I had no philosophical or spiritual objection, I just struggled with the grammar of it all. I don't anymore. Some time ago, I got curious/convicted about using singular plural pronouns in John 3:16. When I inserted the pronouns, I realized they were a better reflection of the fluid multifaceted nature of God and our creation in God's image. We are called to discover the beauty of God beyond the binaries. I think this fluid remix of John 3:16 points us in the right direction. The verse remains in my prayers.

Amen.

FEBRUARY 13, 2016

Lenten Remix 2: The Simple Great Commission

Jesus shouted out, "I got everything you need. Teach love. Do something to seal the deal. Teach them to act like I do. I'll be with you forever."

For such a simple message, the Great Commission/Matt. 28:18–20 is so long. In the midst of the raising from the dead and all, I think something got misquoted. Regardless, I've tried to take the Great Commission down to a simpler form for this Lenten exercise. I think this is the core message of Jesus. Furthermore, I could imagine Jesus shouting these words on the street.

Amen.

FEBRUARY 14, 2016

Lenten Remix 3: Jesus on Truth

"For we will know the truth and the truth will set us free . . ."

In John 8:32, Jesus reveals that truth can't be hidden or bound. The effect of truth is freedom. In this Lenten remix, I take Jesus' original use of singular pronouns and replace them with singular pronoun. Throughout our world, we must remember that our common struggles against injustice must have a common goal . . . truth. There will be no freedom without truth. Our future lies in truth. May we embrace it with all that we are and let the freedom cleanse our souls.

Amen.

FEBRUARY 14, 2016

Lenten Remix 4: The Greatest of These

"In the end, justice, equality and love remain but the greatest of these is love."

The familiar words of 1 Corinthians 13 have grown far too familiar. The words/concepts of faith and hope are used so often that I would argue that the words mean very little in the modern context. In an age desperate for social change, equality and justice feel far more fitting. While love is still the greatest, equality and justice are right there too.

Amen.

FEBRUARY 15, 2016

Lenten Remix 5: Love in Rome

"There is therefore no condemnation for those who are in LOVE."

I've read Romans 8:1 thousands of times. Over and over, the name "Christ Jesus" cut into my flesh like a sword. I think it was because the verse was always used to condemn. If God is love and Jesus is the incarnation of God, then certainly love is a fitting substitute for the name Christ Jesus. Now, I think the verse can reach out to us in love like it was intended to the entire time.

Amen.

FEBRUARY 15, 2016

Boycott the Cooperative Baptist Fellowship!

"Our church voted to leave the Southern Baptist Convention this past Sunday." Overhearing Charlie's comment, I immediately replied, "Why did y'all do something dumb like that?" Even though our whispers were escalating, we hadn't yet caught the attention of our history teacher, Mr. Jones. "Most folks in our church wanted to ordain women." I was absolutely incredulous. "Which one of the liberal denominations did you join?" Charlie looked at me dead in the eyes and said, "THE Cooperative Baptist Fellowship." "Well, you might as well have been handing out free tickets to hell in the process. What's next? Homosexual ordination?" Angered, Charlie shouted, "You'd better take that back. The Cooperative Baptist Fellowship nor our church would ever in a million years ordain no faggots." Mr. Jones raised his head and yelled, "Pipe down or you'll be joining me in detention." When I saw Charlie at our high school reunion a few years ago, he told me that his church was still proudly in the Cooperative Baptist Fellowship and ardently opposed to the participation of gay people in church or denominational life.

"The snow sets this place off." I don't know who I was talking to. I was alone. Maybe, I was talking to God. Maybe, I was just crazy. Who the hell knows? Regardless, The Southern Baptist Theological Seminary is a majestic place. The year was 2007 and the President was one Dr. R. Albert Mohler, Jr. That's right, I was educated within the Southern Baptist Convention long after moderates lost control of the denomination and left. A short time into my tenure, I got a phone call that would change my life. For many years, my mentor served Southern Baptist churches and his last church was affiliated with the Cooperative Baptist Fellowship (CBF). Though he was unquestionably more progressive, I spent many years learning from him. Picking up the phone, I heard the familiar voice of my mentor tell me that he was dying. I traveled through the night to get to him. When I arrived at the house, I walked past his family into his room. Arriving at his bedside, my mentor reached out with his cold sweaty dying hand and told me, "I'm gay and I always have been." Death came quickly thereafter. I knew that he didn't feel comfortable telling any of the churches he served. Though he was a moderate Baptist, my mentor was forced into a closet by the denominations he served. After these events, I grew more progressive by the day and finished Southern as quickly as possible. When I was a student at Emory University someone invited me to be a part of the CBF, I replied that I couldn't be part of a homophobic denomination. This was before I learned of the official homophobic stance of the CBF.

"We're not homophobic!" When you lead with an emphatic denial of homophobia, most of the time that means you're homophobic. A few years ago, an influential member of the CBF led with such a denial. I decided to research further and found an extended history of homophobia. In October of 2000, the Coordinating Council of the CBF adopted the following policy on homosexual behavior related to personnel and funding:

As Baptist Christians, we believe that the foundation of a Christian sexual ethic is faithfulness in marriage between a man and a woman and celibacy in singleness. We also believe in the love and grace of God for all people, both for those who live by this understanding of the biblical standard and those who do not. We treasure the freedom of individual conscience and the autonomy of the local church, and we also believe that congregational leaders should be persons of moral integrity whose lives exemplify the highest standards of Christian conduct and character.

> *Because of this organizational value, the Cooperative Baptist Fellowship does not allow for the expenditure of funds for organizations or causes that condone, advocate or affirm homosexual practice. Neither does this CBF organizational value allow for the purposeful hiring of a staff person or the sending of a missionary who is a practicing homosexual.*

(http://www.cbf.net/media/import/4ff861e3-6f0d-40a0-8eff-dba9c01f884b.pdf)

The phrase "practicing homosexual" is about as homophobic as it gets. When I read this and think about the numerous homophobic experiences I've had with CBF pastors throughout the country, I'm wondering why all these folks left the Southern Baptist Convention in the first place. From recent experiences, I know that most Southern Baptists would be very comfortable with the language that the CBF uses. Maybe the folks in the CBF might be interested in going back?

I decided to take my questions to the leader of the denomination.

When I walked into the gymnasium, I couldn't help but notice how white the room was. While the tables were white, there also wasn't a single person of color in the entire room. The speaker of the hour was CBF Executive Coordinator Suzii Paynter. After listening to her talk about all the stuff that the CBF was doing, the time for questions came. I had to think about it. When I considered the controversial nature of my question, I decided to wait to talk to her after. We'd just exited the church when I asked about the homophobic stances and policies of the CBF. For over ten minutes, Paynter would not answer any of my questions. I remembered something a lawyer friend taught me, when someone refuses to answer a question they have already answered the question. Executive Coordinator Paynter is a defender of the homophobic policies of her homophobic denomination.

Boycott the Cooperative Baptist Fellowship!

Jesus commanded us to "Love our neighbors as our selves." How can you accomplish such a task and have such homophobic policies on the books? It's 2016. There is no reason to be a part of any denomination that functions in this way. On homophobia, the CBF reflects the Southern Baptist Convention far more than it reflects Jesus. Until these homophobic policies are taken off the books and their churches decide to be inclusive spaces, I'm calling on Baptists to boycott the Cooperative Baptist Fellowship. I hope this action brings about the repentance and salvation of our fellow Baptists. Homophobia is not acceptable. In a world desperate for the love of Jesus, there's no reason to partner with or pay for hate. For the sake of all of God's children, boycott!

Amen.

FEBRUARY 16, 2016

Lenten Remix 6: I Never Left

"Surely I never left."

Right at the end of the Bible, Revelation 22:20 is an apocalyptic text. Jesus describes the speed of his return. Verses like this have consistently been used by Christians to channel all of their focus on the impending return of Jesus. I think we need to focus on the fact that Jesus never left.

Amen.

FEBRUARY 17, 2016

Lenten Remix 7: NO Beginning

"There was not a beginning..."

In Genesis 1:1, we are told that there was a beginning. If we are made in the image of God and God is eternal, then our image was always there somewhere. I think the message of scripture points to a lack of a beginning far more than it points to a beginning. We were made in the image of love. Love has always been.

Amen.

FEBRUARY 17, 2016

Lenten Remix 8: The Dying God.

"God comes to die with us."

In the original version of Psalm 46:1, "God is our refuge and strength, an ever-present help in trouble." When I engage the Gospels, I read something different. Jesus comes to be with us so that he might die with us. I think such knowledge makes this verse read very differently.

Amen.

FEBRUARY 19, 2016

Lenten Remix 9: The Screaming Christ

"Jesus screamed."

Upon the death of Lazarus in John 11, "Jesus wept." Often when you lose someone you love, you do more than weep. When I lost my grandmother last year, I screamed. I think Jesus screamed too.

Amen.

FEBRUARY 20, 2016

Lenten Remix 10: The Ass Stones

"Why don't you hypocrites take your stones and shove them up your asses?"

Jesus placing his body in the dirt between the adulterous woman and her accusers is one of the most powerful moments in all of scripture. John relays another powerful moment in 8:32. Jesus looks up from the dirt and says, "Let anyone among you who is without sin be the first to throw a stone at her." The Pharisees walk away. I've often wondered if there was stronger language that Jesus could've used. Enter the modern remix.

Amen.

FEBRUARY 20, 2016

Save Andrew Thomas.

Editor-

Zealous to secure convictions throughout her career, Shelby County District Attorney Amy Weirich has repeatedly abused her power. Don't believe me? Look up the cases of Noura Jackson, Michael Rimmer and Vaern Braswell amongst many others. To that list, I'd like to add the name of Andrew Thomas. In 2000, a Shelby County jury convicted Thomas of the murder of James Day and sentenced him to death. While there were many problems with the way Thomas was prosecuted, there is one fact that stands out. In prosecuting the case Weirich knew that a women named Angela Jackson was paid $750 to testify against Thomas and Weirich knew that Jackson lied about not receiving the payment on the stand. When Thomas first told me, I thought he was full of it. Surely no prosecutor would ever knowingly engage in such unethical behavior? Then, I looked up Weirich's 2011 admission of guilt in US District Court. With Thomas' life on the line, Weirich lied for many years. In the coming weeks, Thomas' appeal is set to go before the United States Court of Appeals for the Sixth Circuit. Instead of seeking to right her wrongs, Weirich is still pushing for Thomas to be executed. Is this the type of person that folks in Shelby County want wildly prosecuting cases and putting further innocent people behind bars? I hope not.

Rev. Dr. Jeff Hood
Spiritual Advisor to Andrew Thomas
Denton, Texas

FEBRUARY 21, 2016

Lenten Remix 11: End Racism

"Love must be sincere. End Racism."

Racism pervades every part of our lives. To deny the systemic nature of racial inequality is to deny love. We must not forget that love must be sincere. In order for love to be sincere we must end racism. In Romans 12:9, Paul tells us to hate what is evil. What could be more evil than racism? You can't follow God and not end racism.

Amen.

FEBRUARY 22, 2016

Lenten Remix 12: Give Your Life

"Give your life."

In John 15:13, Jesus tells the disciples that love doesn't get any greater than sacrificing your life for your friends. We can't have a future worth living in without making the marginalized and oppressed our friends. The message of Jesus is clear. Give your life.

Amen.

FEBRUARY 23, 2016

Lenten Remix 13: I Got This

"I got this."

In Jeremiah 29:11, God declares, "For I know the plans I have for you . . . " I don't need all of that big language. I just need to know that God's got this.

Amen.

FEBRUARY 24, 2016

Lenten Remix 14: Don't Worry

Philippians 4:6 reads, "Do not be anxious about anything . . ." There is an old saying that bubbles up from the islands that has a little better wording for our context, "Don't worry . . ."

Amen.

FEBRUARY 25, 2016

Lenten Remix 15: Just Be Love

In Matthew 22, Jesus tells us to love God and our neighbor. If we are not going to love, our lives our meaningless. People are always talking about what everybody else needs to be. I think we can make Jesus' greatest commandments simpler. Stop worrying about everything else ... Just Be Love.

Amen.

FEBRUARY 26, 2016

Lenten Remix 16: Jesus Had a Vagina

There is not a single verse in all of scripture that describes Jesus' genitalia. Why do we spend so much time assuming that Jesus had a penis? I think our faith would benefit from exploring the femininity of Jesus.

Amen.

FEBRUARY 27, 2016

Lenten Remix 17: Jesus Brought the Wine

In John 2, Jesus brought the wine. How anyone could teach that all alcohol is sinful after reading the verses about the wedding feast? I don't know. I only know that Jesus brought the wine.

Amen.

FEBRUARY 28, 2016

Lenten Remix 18: Loving Your Enemy

"Love the KKK."

Jesus tells us to love our enemies in Matthew 5:44. I can think of few more hateful organizations than the KKK. They are indeed enemies of God. If we are going to love our enemies, we have to love the vilest. We can't follow Jesus without finding a way to love the KKK.

Amen.

FEBRUARY 29, 2016

Lenten Remix 19: The Fake Jesus

"Would you still follow Jesus if Jesus never existed?"

We put a tremendous amount of trust in Matthew, Mark, Luke and John. What if they lied? Would that change your faith in Jesus?

Amen.

MARCH 1, 2016

Lenten Remix 20: Fuck It

"Fuck it."

In Philippians 4:6, Paul doesn't want us to be anxious about anything. I think we should translate that into modern language and approach our anxieties with one phrase in mind . . . Fuck it.

Amen.

MARCH 2, 2016

Lenten Remix 21: The Loving End

"The End is Love"

God is Love. The Beginning was Love. The End is Love. Bring on the Apocalypse.

Amen.

MARCH 3, 2016

Lenten Remix 22: Hate Money!

"Hate Money!"

Paul tells Timothy in 1 Timothy 6:10 that "..the love of money is the root of all evil." Money leads to many evils. We see it everyday. Money is making people sick. Money is ruining lives. Money is killing people. I think Paul should have made it simpler and declared that followers of Jesus should "Hate Money!"

Amen.

MARCH 4, 2016

Lenten Remix 23: Female Disciples

"What happened to the female disciples of Jesus?"

Jesus had many followers. We know that women were amongst them. Why are they mentioned so infrequently in scripture? Why are their stories suppressed? Men have been running the show and writing the narrative since the beginning. What would the female disciples have to say? I think they might show us the way. I imagine they are still speaking.

Amen.

MARCH 5, 2016

Lenten Remix 24: The Genitalia of Jesus

"We don't know anything about Jesus' genitalia."

I've long wondered why people are so certain that Jesus had a penis. The scriptures say nothing about it. Maybe Jesus had a vagina? Maybe Jesus had something much wilder than our current understandings? The bottom line is that we shouldn't assign genitalia to someone when we know anything about their genitalia . . . especially when it comes to God.

Amen.

MARCH 6, 2016

Lenten Remix 25: The Old Testament is Often No Testament

"The Old Testament is often no testament to the love of God."

How many times have you read pieces of the Old Testament and thought it's describing a God you don't know? I struggled with this for so long. Finally, I made a decision that I believed that God is love. Love doesn't do some of the shit that the fake God does in numerous parts of the Old Testament. I believe in Love.

Amen.

MARCH 6, 2016

Boycott the Cooperative Baptist Fellowship! // Uncensored

*There were some concerns from the folks at the CBF about my first posting of this post that led to some censorship. In response, I wanted to make sure that I published the uncensored extended version here.

"Our church voted to leave the Southern Baptist Convention this past Sunday." Overhearing Charlie's comment, I immediately replied, "Why did y'all do something dumb like that?" Even though our whispers were escalating, we hadn't yet caught the attention of our history teacher, Mr. Jones. "Most folks in our church wanted to ordain women." I was absolutely incredulous. "Which one of the liberal denominations did you join?" Charlie looked at me dead in the eyes and said, "THE Cooperative Baptist Fellowship." "Well, you might as well have been handing out free tickets to hell in the process. What's next? Homosexual ordination?" Angered, Charlie shouted, "You'd better take that back. The Cooperative Baptist Fellowship nor our church would ever in a million years ordain no faggots." Mr. Jones raised his head and yelled, "Pipe down or you'll be joining me in detention." When I saw Charlie at our high school reunion a few years ago, he told me that his church was still proudly in the Cooperative Baptist Fellowship and ardently opposed to the participation of gay people in church or denominational life.

The Violence of Being

"The snow sets this place off." I don't know who I was talking to. I was alone. Maybe, I was talking to God. Maybe, I was just crazy. Who the hell knows? Regardless, The Southern Baptist Theological Seminary is a majestic place. The year was 2007 and the President was one Dr. R. Albert Mohler, Jr. That's right, I was educated within the Southern Baptist Convention long after moderates lost control of the denomination and left. A short time into my tenure, I got a phone call that would change my life. For many years, my mentor served Southern Baptist churches and his last church was affiliated with the Cooperative Baptist Fellowship (CBF). Though he was unquestionably more progressive, I spent many years learning from him. Picking up the phone, I heard the familiar voice of my mentor tell me that he was dying. I traveled through the night to get to him. When I arrived at the house, I walked past his family into his room. Arriving at his bedside, my mentor reached out with his cold sweaty dying hand and told me, "I'm gay and I always have been." Death came quickly thereafter. I knew that he didn't feel comfortable telling any of the churches he served. Though he was a moderate Baptist, my mentor was forced into a closet by the denominations he served. After these events, I grew more progressive by the day and finished Southern as quickly as possible. When I was a student at Emory University someone invited me to be a part of the CBF, I replied that I couldn't be part of a homophobic denomination. This was before I learned of the official homophobic stance of the CBF.

"We're not homophobic!" When you lead with an emphatic denial of homophobia, most of the time that means you're homophobic. A few years ago, an influential member of the CBF led with such a denial. I decided to research further and found an extended history of homophobia. In October of 2000, the Coordinating Council of the CBF adopted the following policy on homosexual behavior related to personnel and funding:

As Baptist Christians, we believe that the foundation of a Christian sexual ethic is faithfulness in marriage between a man and a woman and celibacy in singleness. We also believe in the love and grace of God for all people, both for those who live by this understanding of the biblical standard and those who do not. We treasure the freedom of individual conscience and the autonomy of the local church, and we also believe that congregational leaders should be persons of moral integrity whose lives exemplify the highest standards of Christian conduct and character.

Because of this organizational value, the Cooperative Baptist Fellowship does not allow for the expenditure of funds for organizations or causes that condone, advocate or affirm homosexual practice. Neither does this CBF organizational value allow for the purposeful hiring of a staff person or the sending of a missionary who is a practicing homosexual.

(http://www.cbf.net/media/import/4ff861e3-6f0d-40a0-8eff-dba9c01f884b.pdf)

The phrase "practicing homosexual" is about as homophobic as it gets. When I read this and think about the numerous homophobic experiences I've had with CBF pastors throughout the country, I'm wondering why all these folks left the Southern Baptist Convention in the first place. From recent experiences, I know that most Southern Baptists would be very comfortable with the language that the CBF uses. Maybe the folks in the CBF might be interested in going back?

I decided to take my questions to the leader of the denomination.

When I walked into the gymnasium (Spring 2013 CBF luncheon at Agape Baptist Church in Fort Worth, Texas), I couldn't help but notice how white the room was. While the tables were white, there also wasn't a single person of color in the entire room. The speaker of the hour was CBF Executive Coordinator Suzii Paynter. After listening to her talk about all the stuff that the CBF was doing, the time for questions came. I had to think about it. When I considered the controversial nature of my question, I decided to wait to talk to her after. We'd just exited the church when I asked about the homophobic stances and policies of the CBF. For over ten minutes, Paynter would not answer any of my questions. I remembered something a lawyer friend taught me, when someone refuses to answer a question they have already answered the question. Executive Coordinator Paynter is a defender of the homophobic policies of her homophobic denomination.

Jesus commanded us to "Love our neighbors as our selves." How can you accomplish such a task and have such homophobic policies on the books? It's 2016. There is no reason to be a part of any denomination that functions in this way. On homophobia, the CBF reflects the Southern Baptist Convention far more than it reflects Jesus. Until these homophobic policies are taken off the books and their churches decide to be inclusive spaces, I'm calling on Baptists to boycott the Cooperative Baptist Fellowship. I hope this action brings about the repentance and salvation of our fellow Baptists. Homophobia is not acceptable. In a world desperate for the love of Jesus, there's no reason to partner with or pay for hate. For the sake of all of God's children, boycott!

Amen.

MARCH 6, 2016

Madeleine/Lucas: A Poem

Twins
How could it happen again?
We just had sex and now there is 2
More that is
The birth wouldn't arrive
I'll never forget walking your mom in the hallways
Beauty is often slow to begin
Lucas came fast
I loved you from the moment I looked into your eyes
You were a one of a kind surprise
Madeleine delayed
Mom lost blood and scared me to no end
You arrived in the operating room
For a moment I was worried about picking out a tomb
My first girl
How could it be?
I never thought God would be so kind to me
Now here we are
One year later we are still pressing on
You talk
You crawl
You sing
You dance
You smile

The Violence of Being

Oh how I love your smiles
They will carry us more than a million miles
Our love has multiplied and will forevermore
Happy Birthday
Magic is what the future has in store

MARCH 7, 2016

Lenten Remix 26: The Flood

"God didn't destroy the world in a flood."

When I was a child, I struggled to believe that God destroyed the world in a flood. I just didn't find it plausible. The God that I knew and loved would never do such a thing. Now that I have left childish struggles behind and embraced the transformative power of love, I can say with deep assurance, "God didn't destroy the world in a flood."

Amen.

MARCH 8, 2016

Lenten Remix 27: Politicians Killed Jesus

"Would politicians kill Jesus again?"

While I'm sure the world was different then, the leaders who killed Jesus functioned like politicians. Down through the centuries, people have blamed the death of Jesus on religion. I don't think like that. The death of Jesus was about power. The politicians who killed Jesus manipulated the crowds to remove an obstacle. For the last few months, I've watched our politicians in action. The wild scramble for power is scary. Would they kill Jesus again?

Amen.

MARCH 9, 2016

Lenten Remix 28: Seek God

"Seek God."

In Matthew 6:33, we are told, "But seek first *God's* kingdom and his righteousness, and all these things will be given to you as well." Instead of worrying about what is going to be given to us, I think it's best for us to, "Seek God."

Amen.

MARCH 10, 2016

Lenten Remix 29: Beyond Nations

"The only way to follow Jesus is to go to all nations. Once there, we will realize that we have arrived at a place beyond all nations."

References to nations exist throughout scripture. In perhaps the most famous verse of all, Jesus told his followers to go and make disciples of "all nations" (Matt 28:19). When I look around the world today, I see the consequences of our constructions of nations. National borders divide people. National borders keep people from loving their neighbors. National borders keep protecting the resources of the powerful. National borders continue to be about greed. How can we live behind such borders and follow Jesus? I don't think we can. The only way to follow Jesus is to go to all nations. Once there, we will realize that we have arrived at a place beyond all nations.

Amen.

MARCH 11, 2016

Chicken S*it Pastors

There is no greater love than laying down your life for your friends. Jesus didn't mince words in John 15:13. Over the past few days, I've thought about what such words of sacrifice mean in a contemporary context. Then, I made the mistake of thinking about most of the pastors I know. I can only think of one or two who would take their call to follow Jesus seriously enough to give their life for their congregants. The rest are simply chicken shit. When faced with moral conflict, the chicken shit crowd is more worried about losing their standing than doing what is right. When faced with marrying two people of the same sex in violation of the rules of their church, the chicken shit crowd frets over losing their salary or pension. When the world is going to hell, the chicken shit crowd spends all of their time making sure that their own ass is going to be ok. Give their life? These folks won't even give up a little money or institutional connection. The thought of giving their lives has never even crossed their minds. I think it is important that we stay away from these pastors . . . because the person they are following definitely isn't Jesus.

Amen.

MARCH 12, 2016

Lenten Remix 30: The Idolatry of Consequences & Donald Trump

Earlier today in St. Louis, dozens of protestors interrupted Donald Trump and shut down his campaign event for over ten minutes. Tonight, the scene was so chaotic in Chicago that Trump canceled his rally. Watching the chaos unfold, I didn't have to think about where Jesus would be. The hate that has regularly flowed out of Trump makes him a very similar figure to the Pharisees of Jesus' day. Instead of worrying about the consequences, Jesus confronted hate and injustice where he found it. There is a lesson here for us. Instead of worrying about the consequences, we have the responsibility to confront hate and injustice where we find it. There is no question where followers of Jesus should be right now . . . shutting down these Trump rallies.

Amen.

MARCH 13, 2016

Lenten Remix 31: Hell Exists and It's Here

*I created the above hand depiction of the thoughts of this article.

I refused to engage. The finer points of theology have never been all that interesting to me. Then, an argument about hell bubbled up. The liberals argued that hell didn't exist. The conservatives declared that hell was central to our faith. I'd had enough. Rising, I said, "To declare that hell is central to our faith is to deny the redemptive work of Jesus. To deny that hell exists is to deny the hell that our neighbors are living in everyday. Hell exists and it's here. Instead of talking about hell, we should be trying to pull people out of it."

Amen.

MARCH 14, 2016

Lenten Remix 32: Politics is Not Our Faith

Politics is not our faith. Hillary Clinton is not God. Donald Trump is not God. Ted Cruz is not God. Bernie Sanders is not God. Only God is God. Vote for God.

Amen.

MARCH 15, 2016

Lenten Remix 33: Jesus Didn't Have to Die

Before Jesus died, Jesus was the way. If Jesus hadn't died, Jesus would still be the way. In the midst of his anguish, Jesus chose to die to show us the way. Could Jesus have shown us the way in another way? I think so. No matter what he chose to do, Jesus was and is the way. Jesus didn't have to die. Jesus did die.

Amen.

MARCH 16, 2016

Lenten Remix 34: The Nocturnal Emissions of Jesus

We must stop denying the humanity of Jesus by neglecting the fullness of his humanity! Jesus was human. Jesus had nocturnal emissions. While I don't want to spend much time speculating on the contents of any divine dreams, I think affirmation of the fullness of Jesus' humanity is what helps us affirm the fullness of our own humanity.

Amen.

MARCH 16, 2016

When a Black Cop Kills an Unarmed Child

Here in Texas, justice is swift and injustice is too. When violence happens, one has to pay close attention to make sure they know the difference.

Farmers Branch is known for injustice. Persons of color don't get a fair shake within the city limits. Not too far up the road, there is a city called Addison. Things function similarly there. This is where the murder went down.

Farmers Branch police officer Ken Johnson was working as a security guard when he came across Jose Cruz running out of an apartment and jumping in a nice car. Assuming that he was committing multiple crimes, Johnson chased him down and shot him dead at an intersection. Jose Cruz was 16. From every account, Cruz was also unarmed. This afternoon, the Addison Police Department announced that Johnson was being indicted for murder.

I couldn't believe it.

Those of us who struggle against police brutality in Texas don't often get victories. The only problem with celebrating is that Ken Johnson is black. Locally, much of the activist community was questioning why Johnson was charged so fast. While I respect the complexities of the question, I feel like someone who shoots an

The Violence of Being

unarmed child dead in the street should be charged with murder as quickly as possible. Frankly, I'm glad that Johnson was charged and I wished they'd charged him sooner. I'm tired of cops killing people. When a black cop kills an unarmed child, they deserve to go to jail not to be the beneficiaries of our protective impulses. They are hired to protect us and I don't know why we spend so much time protecting them. A cop who kills is still a killer no matter what the color of their skin is. Killer cops should be indicted as quickly as possible.

Amen.

MARCH 17, 2016

Lenten Remix 35: The Heresy of Conversation

When faced with a woman's impending execution, Jesus got down in the dirt with her. If the stones had flown, Jesus would've died. Jesus didn't entertain any conversation. Jesus remained silent and got down in the dirt. In our culture, we keep seeing people thrown in the dirt. Instead of joining the oppressed and marginalized, we keep asking for more conversation. We don't believe in following Jesus. We believe in conversation. We are heretics.

Amen.

MARCH 18, 2016

Lenten Remix 36: The Money Changers

Jesus was enraged. The money changers were ripping off the poorest in the community. Jesus kicked them out. Why don't we respond similarly? Is there any difference between the money changers and the payday lenders in our communities? I don't think so. Where is our rage?

Amen.

MARCH 20, 2016

Letter to the Editor Before the Execution of Adam Ward

To the editor:

What are we doing?

We are a bloodthirsty people. We can't even get through Holy Week. Instead of remembering the execution of Jesus, we're preparing to execute Adam Ward. In 2005, Ward murdered City of Commerce Code Enforcement Officer Michael "Pee Wee" Walker. In 2016, we are preparing to do the same.

Just like Pilate, many will try to absolve their responsibility for this premeditated murder. Instead of using water basin, we just keep dehumanizing the condemned until we feel good about killing them. Loving your neighbor as your self doesn't work like that.

Our screams for blood and vengeance must be similar to the cries that Jesus heard before his execution. Our actions are similar too. We're carrying him to the execution chamber. We're strapping him to the gurney. We're injecting the poison. This is how evil people celebrate Holy Week. We reenact the execution.
I'm praying for some Holy Week conversions.

I'm praying we get saved from our addiction to executions.

The Violence of Being

I'm praying...

Put down the needle Texas!

Amen.

MARCH 21, 2016

The Blood: A Holy Week Execution

"There is a fountain filled with blood drawn from Emmanuel's veins; and sinners plunged beneath that flood lose all their guilty stains."

We sang it over and over. As the organ played, fear kept creeping in. The night before, my cousin showed me one of the *A Nightmare on Elm Street* movies. Sweat dripped from my face. With every line, I grew more frightened. The preacher paused the music and declared, "God murdered his son to satisfy his wrath for your guilt. Blood is the only way out of here alive!" Scenes from the movie kept rushing back. God chased his son down a corridor. Knives extended from God's fingers. Reaching the corner, God slashed until his son was dead. Shouting out, I rushed to the front. I had to get out of the way of Freddy Krueger or the God that murdered his own son. One of the pastors met me. Immediately, I prayed, "God, I'm a sinner. Don't take my blood! I trust in Jesus!" As tears streamed down my face, the pastor assured me that the blood was enough to protect me. I never believed him. If God was capable of murdering his own son, God was capable of anything.

True liberation only comes from the death of childish ideas. There once was a man named Paul. Before he met God, Paul believed that his mission in life was to run around killing folks. Paul believed that blood was the only path to what he wanted. Finally,

God interrupted Paul's childish thinking with a dose of love. After he got saved, Paul wrote these words, "When the perfect comes, the partial is done away with. When I was a child, I spoke like a child, I understood as a child, I thought as a child; but when I grew up, I put away childish things." Only children deal in blood. Grownups deal in love.

Originating in our thirst for blood, the death penalty represents a failure to love. I don't think it's a coincidence that the highest executing states in our nation all have heavily Christian populations. Deadly theology leads to deadly practice. The death penalty is based on an idea that blood is required to atone for evil. We are carrying out an ancient ritual of atonement every time the state kills for us. The problem is that this denies any belief that Jesus is the atonement. God didn't kill Jesus. The love of Jesus is what took him to the cross. The atonement is love. How can we love and kill at the same time? We can't. Every time we carry out one of these executions we deny the love of Jesus. The death penalty has made us heretics. We are desperately in need of salvation.

Here in Texas, we are reenacting Holy Week. The only difference is that Adam Ward is not Jesus. We are letting Ward say goodbye to his friends. We are giving Ward his final meal. We are leading Ward to the place. We are forcing Ward to climb up. We are making Ward extend his arms. We are forcing metal to pierce Ward's skin.

We are pumping poison into Ward's veins. We are murderers. There is no question that Ward murdered City of Commerce Code Enforcement Officer Michael "Pee Wee" Walker in 2005. There is also no question that we are about to do the same thing.

Blood doesn't help. Over and over, I put my faith in blood. No matter how many times I prayed, I got nowhere. The same is true of these executions. We can keep shedding blood all we want, but it won't get us anywhere. Our image of God must change. God is about restoration not execution. We must let go of the fear before the love can pour in. God is here to save not to kill. God is here to give power to blood. In the midst of the demand for blood, the power flows through sacrificing our blood for others. Jesus showed us that this is the greatest path. On this day, that path flows through Adam Ward.

"There is a fountain filled with blood drawn from Adam Ward's veins; and sinners plunged beneath that flood lose all their guilty stains."

Amen.

MARCH 21, 2016

Crazy Like Me: A Holy Week Execution

Walking home that night, I knew something wasn't right. Paranoia filled my brain. Panic filled my heart. Anxiety filled my stomach. Danger was everywhere. In the darkness, someone kept whispering my name. I begged them to stop. They laughed at me. No one was there. Closing my eyes, I raced down the sidewalk. Repeatedly, I felt people pulling and grabbing at me. Running full speed, I couldn't get to my dorm fast enough. When I opened the door, I saw evil incarnate in the form of the night guard. Feeling something in my pants, I knew I'd shit myself. Tears streamed down my face. "Get away from me!" I screamed. When I got to my room, I jumped in the bed. For hours, the demons tried to smother me. Waking up the next morning, I couldn't believe how destroyed my room was. I knew I did it. This wasn't the first time. Four years later, I was diagnosed with bipolar disorder.

Code enforcement in Commerce, Texas received complaint after complaint concerning the home that Adam Ward shared with his dad. The department cited the Wards repeatedly. When Michael Walker arrived at the Ward home, there was no reason to believe that he would be doing anything other than performing the routine duties of a code enforcement officer. When Walker started taking pictures of violations, he didn't know that Adam Ward was suffering from delusions about the local government trying to kill him. Diagnosed with bipolar disorder when he was 4, Ward was spiraling. Ward began to argue with Walker. When Walker said that he was calling for back up, Ward's delusions told him that he was as good as dead. Running inside, Ward grabbed a gun. Without saying much, Ward ran at Walker and shot him nine times. Though Ward claimed that Walker had a gun too, there was never any evidence to prove it. The delusions haven't stopped. Ward was and is mentally ill.

Over the years, I've chosen to not own a gun. I've never felt healthy enough. I wish that Adam Ward had made the same choice. Maybe he was incapable of such decisions. Regardless, I know how quickly one can spiral out of control. I know what it looks like to be so paranoid and delusional that there is no way for you to be responsible for your actions. Ward is crazy like me. We are sick. There is no cure for our disease. While I have found a regiment of medicine that works pretty good for me, I know that the pills can only do so much. There are times when reality seems difficult to grasp. I don't know where Ward was with treatment. I only know that he was very sick. In Matthew 25, Jesus says that he is with the sick. Tonight, the State of Texas will try to execute Adam Ward. I know that Jesus will be there with him in his sickness. Jesus is always placing his body between the sick and those who seek their demise. We should too.

Throughout the day, I will travel to the execution chamber in Huntsville. Instead of commemorating Holy Week in a place of worship, I've chosen to experience the passion of Jesus in Adam Ward. When the State of Texas places the lethal needle into Ward's arm, I will be standing outside in defiance. We all know that Ward's actions aren't any crazier than the execution we are planning tonight. We think we can teach people not to kill by killing. Who's more delusional: Ward or us?

Amen.

MARCH 23, 2016

Lenten Remix 37: Jesus is the Stranger

Jesus declared himself to be present in the strangers amongst us. Why do we keep deporting the strangers amongst us?

Amen.

MARCH 23, 2016

Lenten Remix 38: Dying

Jesus died. Why are we so afraid of the dying?

Amen.

MARCH 23, 2016

Lenten Remix 39: Jesus is Hungry

Jesus declared himself to be present in the hungry. Why are we so stingy with our food?

Amen.

MARCH 23, 2016

Lenten Remix 40: Living

The resurrection is about living beyond death. Live like you believe it.

Amen.

MARCH 24, 2016

The Resurrection of Ms. Shade Schuler

Adapted from a post from August 2015.

Less than a hundred feet from residences, local authorities discovered the badly decomposed body of a transgender woman of color. The Dallas Police Department put out a detailed description of the body and asked for help. For weeks, no one seemed to know who this woman was. When the woman was finally identified as 22-year-old Ms. Shade Schuler, I realized that she belonged to no one . . . she was forgotten.

In the twilight of that August 2015 night, the heat was excruciating. With every breath, I sweated through my shirt. The jokes of children filled the air. I laughed too. When we stepped onto the hidden gravel road, things got real. I knew we were on holy ground. No one spoke much. Everyone just seemed to be concentrating on the next step. The smell lingered. The heat didn't stop. I worried that the bread and chalice would slip out of my hands. The screech startled me. Perhaps, the bird was warning us that we were nearing the point of no return. I assumed it was an old fire pit. When I saw the black spot was in the shape of a body, I knew better.

The presence of God was unmistakable. When Carmarion Anderson and I lifted up the elements to the heavens, there was electricity flowing in the air. We remembered the oppression she faced in life.

The Resurrection of Ms. Shade Schuler

We remembered her murder. In the transcendence of the moment, we knew that she never died. "This is the body and blood of Ms. Shade." Bending down to touch the spot, everything stopped and Jesus whispered softly in my ear, "What you have done to the least of these you have done to me . . . " Looking at that empty spot on the ground, I believed the words as much as I ever had.

God never forgot about her. God never called her names. God never believed that she didn't have value. God was in her. I know. I met God there.

I believe in the resurrection of Ms. Shade Schuler.

Amen.

APRIL 7, 2016

A Powerful Word

"Da-Da!" No sweeter word has ever hit my ears. In the midst of the chaos, my son looked at me and called out to me with his first word. Each time we send word to the great beyond, I know God feels the same way.

Amen.

APRIL 8, 2016

The Execution:
In Pragmatic Verse

Fear was all I knew
Every step drew me closer
The line taunted me
I refused to stop
I forced every step
Backing down was not an option

Every thump in my chest
Every knot in my stomach
Every lump in my throat
I felt

I stood
I stared
I refused
To move

Their God is the devil
Until the execution was over
I stared him down
I'll be back

Amen.

APRIL 9, 2016

Fifty Years after the Death of God: Learning to Kill

"God is dead. God remains dead. And we have killed him."

—Friedrich Nietzsche, *The Gay Science*, Section 125, tr. Walter Kaufmann

Every syllable reverberated loudly in my ears. In a scene wildly reminiscent of one of these *God's Not Dead* movies, my philosophy professor stood his tallest and shouted Nietzsche's words repeatedly at the front of our classroom. Sensing our fear, he demanded a response. I waited for someone to try to resurrect God. After a few uncomfortable seconds, a big guy on the other side of the room farted as loud as I'd ever heard anyone fart. The walls and windows seemed to shake. There was only one person who didn't laugh, our professor. Looking back, I don't know if it was the wind or the smell that broke up his attempt to assassinate any faith remaining in the room. I only know that mine was damaged. For many years, I ruminated on Nietzsche's words. I'm glad I did. Presently, they form the basis of my faith.

Fifty years have passed since Time Magazine asked the question, "Is God Dead?" on their infamous April 8, 1966 cover. The question arose out of a desire to explain the growing uselessness of the idea of God in a modern age. The provocative cover words were a reference to Nietzsche's claim that God was dead. I was browsing through a history book when I saw the red and black cover for the first time. Ferociously searching online, I found the accompanying article, "Toward a Hidden God." My theology would never be the same.

Leaning in to engage deeply, I read the article multiple times. Though writer John Elson identified US Christian professors Thomas J.J. Altizer, William Hamilton and Paul Van Buren as the primary leaders of the Death of God movement, I later realized that French philosopher Gabriel Vahanian and Jewish theologian Richard Rubenstein were also highly influential. The influence of Paul Tillich on the movement is also worth noting. In their collective audacity to declare God dead, the Death of God thinkers unintentionally made room for the resurrection of God.

People don't realize that God has to die before a God worth believing in can be resurrected. I read as many works connected to the Death of God movement as I could get my hands on. For the first time in my life, I realized that a dead God might be the only path to the real God. When my mind journeyed back to my philosophy professor's Nietzsche stand, I was grateful. I realized that those were the words I needed. Thinking deeper, I knew that evangelism had to do with killing. If we're going to search for the resurrected God, we must become experts at killing.

Since God is always beyond the God that we can conceive of, it is evil to not be about the killing of God. In our faith, death and resurrection go together. Liberation isn't possible without some God killing.

The liberation theologians that followed the Death of God movement understood the importance of killing God. James Cone could not have resurrected the blackness of God without the slaughter of a white God. Rosemary Radford Ruether or Mary Daly could not have resurrected the feminine God without the slaughter of the male God. Gustavo Gutiérrez could not have resurrected the poor God without the slaughter of the rich God. Nancy Eiesland could not have resurrected a disabled God without the slaughter of the abled God. The names and ideas are endless. Though these theologians are far from perfect, there is no question that they each represent significant movements in theology that would not have been possible without the boldness of the Death of God movement. The idea that we can kill God is foundational to liberation thought and practice. In the midst of our age of marginalization and injustice, we need new killers.

Baptists used to be a bold people. Baptists were willing to drown rather than give up their beliefs. Baptists used to give their lives to the poor. Baptists fought and died for the civil rights of others. Baptists used to be a bold people. Now, Baptists are on the wrong side of nearly every major social issue of our time. How could such boldness die? Baptists lost their killer instinct. Baptists traded the danger of the mystery of God for the safety of the certainty of false constructions of God. If your church is homophobic, kill your homophobic God. If your church is racist, kill your racist God. If your church is sexist, kill your sexist God. Baptists need to get back to killing.

Resurrection is always the promise for the theological killer. Death does not get the final answer. Looking back at the Death of God movement, I am reminded of our responsibility to be serial killers in search of the God beyond God. In the words of Nietzsche, may we all stand together and proclaim for the future of our church, "God is dead . . . we have killed him." The resurrection won't be far behind.

Amen.

APRIL 10, 2016

Memories

Beatings.
Drinks.
Flowed together.
Was it a fist?
Was it a laugh?
Who knows?
I know I got it hit hard.
Repeatedly.
The pain lingers.

APRIL 22, 2016

Her name is Amy Francis-Joyner

I love Prince. We experienced the loss of a true cultural icon this week. We also experienced another great loss.

Earlier this week, Howard High School of Technology in Wilmington, Delaware was the site of a fight. This was a planned confrontation. Before school began, a couple of girls met in the bathroom. Words were exchanged. Fists started to fly. Chaos erupted. One of the young ladies hit her head on the sink. The girls kept pummeling. The blood kept flowing. The fight ended with a body lying dead on the ground.

Her name is Amy Francis-Joyner. Our addiction to violence killed her. We put our kids in superhero underwear. We promote violent cartoons. We let our kids watch wrestling. We teach our kids that good always wins by force. We laugh at violent online videos. We don't love God. We love violence. We are an evil people who deny the love of God with every piece of violence that we entertain. It should come as no surprise that no one cares about the death of a child at the hands of other children.

Her name is Amy Francis-Joyner.

Amen.

APRIL 24, 2006

Max Soffar is Alive and We're Dead

In 2014, I put together a letter from an influential group of Baptists asking the Texas Board of Pardons and Paroles for clemency for terminally ill death row inmate Max Soffar (included below). There were many questions about his guilt then. There are even more questions now. Unfortunately, Max Soffar died of cancer this evening around 5pm without ever getting the chance to prove his innocence. I know that he's with God. I'm more worried about us.

> Baptists for Alternatives to the Death Penalty
> 2709 S Lamar Blvd #109, Austin, TX 78704

Texas Board of Pardons and Paroles
Clemency Section
General Counsel's Office
8610 Shoal Creek Boulevard
Austin, TX 78758

Dear Members of the Texas Board of Pardons and Paroles,

"Blessed are the merciful, for they will be shown mercy." Jesus spoke these words in the Sermon on the Mount. We would imagine this is probably not the first time that a bunch of preachers have written to you and used such language. Regardless of the frequency of their use, these powerful words from Matthew 5:7

The Violence of Being

should never become mundane. Jesus directly connects our capacity to show mercy with the mercy that will be shown to us.

We ask that you close your eyes and think with us for a moment. Imagine you have spent 34 years of nights trying to figure out how to prove that you did not commit a crime. Imagine questioning God and humanity day in and day out. Imagine just when you think that your lawyers have found the evidence that will exonerate you and set you free . . . you are told you are dying of liver cancer and will not live to see your innocence proven. This is the case of Max Soffar #685. This is why we are writing to ask that you open your hearts and extend mercy.

Time is short. We know that you are the only people on the planet who can help Max Stoffar #685 and let him die in peace. We ask you to extend the level of mercy that you would hope to be extended to you. For we never know when we will need the mercy of another.

Baptists for Alternatives to the Death Penalty

APRIL 25, 2016

The Last Verdict: A Book Review

Arpin-Ricci, Jamie. The Last Verdict. Self-Published. 2016. http://www.amazon.com/Last-Verdict-Jamie-Arpin-Ricci/dp/1523952687

I get solicitations for reviews and endorsements all the time. Most, I have to ignore. If I responded to everybody, I wouldn't get any of my writing done. So when Jamie Arpin-Ricci messaged me about his book *The Last Verdict*, I was skeptical at best. After multiple exchanges, I sent Arpin-Ricci my address. In my mind, I guess I was thinking that I could read a few paragraphs and toss it out. When the book arrived, I avoided it. Yesterday, I sat down to read ready to quickly get back up. Hell, I didn't even know the damn thing was a novel until the first page. Shockingly, I read every word in one sitting. Few books have ever moved me the way that this one did.

I don't have to wait for what else comes out. This is the most creative book of the year on the death penalty.

"What does one wear to an execution?" (1) The haunting first question stalked me on every remaining page. This is the story of two women struggling with what to put on both literally and metaphorically in the light of the horrors of the death penalty. Alice Goodman loses her daughter Maddy to a terrible murder. For eighteen years, Goodman fights to have Mark Williams executed for the crime. Ultimately, Goodman is successful. Goodman's barrage of emotions hit you from every angle. Most stories would end there. Boldly, Arpin-Ricci pushes ahead. Lori Williams is the "Monster's Mother" (33). Williams loses her son Mark to a terrible tragedy. For eighteen years, Williams struggles with slowly losing her son. In the end, Williams is in the chamber when her son is executed. Williams' barrage of emotions hit you from every angle. In the midst of the pain of it all, the interweaving narratives of Goodman and Williams grabbed me and pulled at me in ways I never anticipated.

While I certainly don't want to give away any twists of plot, I would be remiss if I didn't talk about the magic of the final pages of *The Last Verdict*. With every sentence, Arpin-Ricci becomes a grander and grander magician. The narrative changed and transformed me. I couldn't believe what was happening. Through it all, I was brought face to face with the eternal power of love and grace in the land of the living. I read the final few lines with gusto. "And then, I reach out and take her hand in mine just for a moment. And that gulf between us closes-not completely, but enough" (55). I was so deeply touched that I threw the book up in the air in jubilation. *The Last Verdict* is now my go to title when people ask me to recommend a book about the death penalty.

Rev. Dr. Jeff Hood

MAY 8, 2016

My Flock

We're never able to find underwear for our children. Truthfully, even if we bought a couple hundred pair, they'd still find places to hide. When the unthinkable happens and two clean pair of underwear surface, we lift our heads to the sky and give thanks to God. Our oldest two children just turned four. They are still practicing their underwear expertise. One morning, I was reminded of their lack of complete knowledge. Rushing to get in the car, I probably didn't remind my oldest to go to the bathroom before we departed. A few miles from our home, I heard the call, "Daddy!" When I looked back, I had to remind myself that there was no need to get pissed off about urine exploding all over your previously clean child. When we arrived for the service, I took some wipes and did the best I could. Thankfully, there was a pair of clean underwear in the diaper bag. I expected everything to be ok. Church is supposed to be a place of radical hospitality right? The childcare worker was on a different page and coarsely told me, "We don't let children run around in their underwear." With my child in arm, I proceeded into the sanctuary. I knew it was only going to get worse.

The liturgy was the same. The prayers were the same. The music was the same. The same was even the same. For half the service, I sat there and thought about how irrelevant all this shit was. Holding tightly to my child, I started to think about the future. "Is this what I want my children to know about God?" I started to twitch. God is hungry. God is thirsty. God is a stranger. God is naked. God is sick. God is in prison. The twitch became an itch. I knew that I was betraying everything I knew about God by remaining in the institutional church. God has never been in these spaces. God is always in the streets. I've never had a problem meeting God there. So, why do I feel the need to be a part of the institutional church? I guess I figured I needed a flock. When the familiar words hit I was done,

"All creatures of our God and King
Lift up your voice and with us sing,
Alleluia! Alleluia!"

Please, make no mistake . . . I think the song is beautiful. The problem is that the song doesn't speak to our reality. I got up and walked out. When I pushed through the doors, there were two words that stayed with me, "All creatures."

For a few days, I pondered what it would all mean. How in the hell does an ordained minister leave the institutional church? In time, I realized that I walked out of the institutional doors to step into the real church. I keep finding God in my street activism and theologizing. With that said, I did miss having a flock. So, I bought some chickens.

Riding up to the feed store, I prayed. These were not the same old prayers. I prayed that God would teach me what to feed the chickens. I prayed that God would teach me to house the chickens. I prayed that God would teach me how to love the chickens. I prayed that God would help me not to kill the chickens. After praying for a moment more, I realized that some real human and humane prayers were surfacing when I started oscillating the words "people" and "chickens." Nevertheless, I bought three red chickens, three black chickens, two white chickens and two brown chickens. Before we got in the car, one of the red ones scratched me and one of the black ones pooped through a hole in the bottom of the box. No matter what happened, I just got happier and happier. I knew that there was something very spiritual going on.

My Flock

To say that I fell in love is an understatement. God is love. Since I fell deeply in love with the chickens, I realized that God sometimes had a beak and feathers. From the moment I brought them home, I knew I'd found my flock.

I had no idea what to do with chickens. I just kept going through the improvised process I envisioned one step at a time. I need to house them. I need to feed them. I need to water them. I need to make sure they are healthy. I need to let them out to range. The more I went through the process, the more I realized that the chickens were teaching me. I need to house people. I need to feed people. I need to give people drink. I need to make sure people are healthy. I need to help people be free. The chickens keep teaching me. Don't step in shit. Be gentle. Watch where you're going. We meet for church every morning. I find my flock to be so much more spiritual than the flock I used to meet at the institutional church.

To those who think I'm crazy, I really don't give a flock.

This morning my flock and I prepared a beautiful prayer just for you,

"God, please be with all of those people too chicken to find God outside the walls of a church."

Amen.

MAY 8, 2016

no surrender :
an ode to Emily

we never planned
we just did
no looking back
the test said yes
what a mess
there's two
what do we do
no retreat
life changed
more to explain
slowly we grew
all i needed was you
no hesitation
one more child
nothing the same
three children
to maintain
then more news
another two
no distractions
the screams
the pain
life changed
no substitutions

NO SURRENDER : AN ODE TO EMILY

five children
too much
not for you
you just do
what you do
you are mom
no surrender

MAY 22, 2016

From the Party

As you eat the cupcakes . . .

We were shocked
We didn't know what to do
We only knew that we loved you
Your mother pushed
I tried
I was best at staying by her side
Time flew
The day arrived
We didn't know what was in store
We'd had a few false starts before
We waited for hours
Your mother pushed
The time finally came
Nothing was ever going to be the same
Jeff came out quick
Phillip was sick
They said you couldn't breath
It terrified me
Seven days later you were finally free
Life is magical when we're with you
4 Years Old!
We marvel at how you've grown

Now . . .

From the Party

Back to the party.

-Dad

MAY 26, 2016

The Dream: A Vision of Our Reality

Last night, I had a vivid dream.

The pain of the dream is still with me this morning.

I was in a waiting room. There were all sorts of people everywhere. We were told to be quiet. We were told to not cause any commotion. We were told to wait our turn. No one would tell us what we were waiting for. Then, my name was called. I went up to the desk. Quietly, I was informed that I was dying. Then, I was asked to sign a paper to hasten my death. When I looked back to the waiting room, I realized that we were all waiting on death. We were all stripped of our individuality in the process. The institution was our undertaker and we were expected to be it's willing subjects.

Last night, I believe I had a vision from God.

Institutions flood our lives. Institutions govern us. We shop at institutions. Institutions educate us. We worship at institutions. Institutions are the center of healthcare. I could go on all day. When you consider how deeply institutions are immersed in our lives, you realize how institutions are guiding us from death to death. Institutions are constantly killing our individuality. Institutions allow no room for people to be who they are. Institutions are killing us. Everyone is expected to go from institution to institution and wait their turn to die.

This morning, I started to dream of a way forward.

God created us to be unique in God's image. The path forward is to push back against the normativity that is constantly suffocating our individuality. We must be the queer individuals that God created us to be in the first place. We must step out of line. We must never sit quietly and wait to die. This is our time. This is our moment. Death has no power over us.

This is the moment were I run back into the waiting room screaming.
This is the moment where people wake up.
This is the moment where people start kicking open doors.
This is the moment where people are set free.

Amen.

MAY 27, 2016

The Slap

Sitting on a park bench . . .
I saw a woman slap her child tonight.
The offense was hitting another child.
I watched the little girl take it.
What else was she supposed to do?
Before I could react . . .
They were gone.
Peace seems impossible.
You can't teach a child not to hit by hitting.

MAY 28, 2016

The United States Flag at the Front of the Church is Blasphemous

A United States soldier processed the flag of the United States of America in to our sanctuary as we stood at attention singing "God Bless America." The veterans in our midst were honored as we sang the "Star Spangled Banner." The "Battle Hymn of the Republic" proceeded the pastor's fiery sermon on the coming destruction of our beloved nation if we " . . . did not turn from our wicked ways." Somehow gays, abortion and popular culture always made it into these services . . . but that is another story. The service concluded with an invitation to salvation as the congregation sang "God of Our Fathers." To say that the services of my Baptist youth were precariously wrapped in nationalism is an understatement . . . we believed that God's military was the United States military. Despite the fact that we did so much else that was problematic, my mind remains focused on the United States flag on that gold stand up on the altar.

In many Memorial Day services throughout our nation, some of those who have fallen victim to our thirst for violence and power will be honored and celebrated. We will remember the soldiers and attempt to reconcile their sacrifice with our faith. Unfortunately, there will be little conversation about peace and preventing the deaths of any one else. There will be no conversation of the millions and millions of people who have died as a result of our failed foreign policies and military interventions. The words of Jesus will be forgotten amidst the words of patriotism and nationalism.

No one will recite Jesus' words in Matthew 26:52, " . . . those who live by the sword will die by the sword." Matthew 5:44 and Jesus' reminder to "love our enemies and pray for those who persecute us" will not make an appearance. Least of all will we remember the millions and millions of people who have died in places with names like Hiroshima, Hanoi, Waziristan, Nagasaki, Kabul and Baghdad in the infernos created by our bombs . . . those "least of these" dead because we failed to see Jesus in their midst. No these words won't be remembered . . . and I know most congregations won't be talking beyond the soldiers who have died and will miss the opportunity to have a conversation about the wider call of Jesus to peace and justice.

My mind wonders back to that flag though. To put the United States flag on the altar of a church is to insinuate that somehow the United States has a claim to the grace of God that other nations and peoples do not. To put the United States flag at the front blurs that glorious declaration "For God so loved the world . . . " Can you imagine what someone from another country thinks when they see that United States flag up front at our churches? There is no nationality barrier to the altar of God. Jesus does not love the United States more than any other nation . . . to put a flag at the front and bless the atrocities committed by an incredibly powerful people in the name of Jesus is blasphemous.

A real conversation about the non-violent love of Jesus and our purpose as followers can only happen when we take down the United States flags in our sanctuaries that stand in the way. If we want to truly honor slain soldiers we will stop perpetuating the nationalism that killed them. So let's toss out all the flags and have a real Memorial Day next year . . . one that memorializes and celebrates a time when we began to emulate Jesus' love for all people

Flag at the Front of the Church is Blasphemous

and put to death the nationalism that fooled us into thinking that violence can bring about peace.

Amen.

MAY 29, 2016

A Memorial Day Prayer

Oh False God That We Call America
Unhallowed Is Your Name
You Help Us Kill And Assert Our Will
On Earth As We Think It Is In Heaven

Oh One True God, Save Us From This Bullshit
Give Us This Day Our Daily Brains
Forgive Us For Killing Our Enemies
As We Forgive Those Who Kill Our Friends

Lead Us Not Into The Temptation of Nationalism
For Thou Is The Destroyer Of Our Patriotism
Now and Forever

Amen.

JUNE 1, 2016

The Death of Heroes and The Divinity of Difference

Most people don't know that I love comics. For a long time, I was scared to tell people. How can anyone be a serious scholar when they fill their minds with illustrated boxes and word bubbles? I don't care about the questions of dumbasses anymore. I've learned to just be. Furthermore, I've learned to find God in the magic of those flimsy little books. Truthfully, I find few things more intellectually stimulating than sitting in our backyard surrounded by chickens, reading a classic edition of X-Men and scribbling in my little black notebook the thoughts that come to mind.

I love X-Men above all others. The clash between mutants and humans reveals much about the nature of life. No one seems to have the ability to just stop and accept the fact that difference is the only way to make a difference. The constant battles for civil rights that take place in the pages of X-Men have always informed my work. The X-Men have helped me to understand death as well. When Jean Grey (Phoenix) died in *The Uncanny X-Men* #136, I realized that heroes die.

The death of heroes causes us to martyrize them as quickly as possible. I think that we're scared that our dead heroes will be forgotten. Do you think that Jesus would have been remembered if Jesus had never died? I doubt it. We are never able to leave our heroes dead. We have to resurrect them. The problem with such thinking is that we forget that there is life in death.

There is no such thing as heroes. There is only us and the life we are able to find in death. I follow the X-Men because they constantly remind me that there is life in death. The story always continues.

In the end, there is only death. In the end, there is only life. In death is life. In life is death. What's the difference? There is no difference of category. There is only each of us. We are life and death. We are the difference of person.

The X-Men taught me about the futility of life and the divinity of difference.

Amen.

JUNE 2, 2016

On Silence

Growing up, I was told that I needed to have a daily time of silence.
In college, I was told I needed to meet God in the silence.
In seminary, I was told that silence is a spiritual discipline.
Now, I'm told that silence should be at the core of my spiritual life.
Please, shut the fuck up.
In our age of injustice, the only way to follow God is to speak up.
We don't need more silence.

Amen.

JUNE 4, 2016

God Isn't the Cure

There was an old white Mitsubishi television in the corner of our kitchen. Dad gave it to Mom one Christmas. Despite the efforts of my teacher to keep my attention, I dreamed of that television all day long. Once the dismissal bell rang, I raced home. The Mighty Morphin Power Rangers were all that I cared about. I was a little manic about the show. I opened the door before the car came to a complete stop. Once inside, I grabbed one of our heavy wooden chairs and pulled it as close to the television as I could get it. When I heard the Mighty Morphin Power Rangers theme song, I knew it was time. A few minutes into the show, the television started flickering. Then, the old Mitsubishi television cut off completely. My Mom couldn't fix it. After another few minutes, the television came back on. The only problem was that only one channel worked. The Trinity Broadcasting Network was my only source of afternoon entertainment. I thought it was going to be boring until a guy named Benny Hinn came on.

I was glued to the television. Bodies kept hitting the floor. People kept on shaking. Everybody had their eyes closed. Hands waved back and forth to the rhythm of the beat. I'd never seen anything like it. I loved that shit. Benny Hinn was my new favorite preacher. Instead of the Mighty Morphin Power Rangers, I started tuning in to Hinn. Who needs superheroes when you have a man running around on a stage knocking people over with just the power of God in his fingertips? For many months, I practiced on anyone who would let me. When I wasn't able to do it like Hinn, I simply figured that I didn't have enough faith. Regardless, I kept watching and trying for a number of years. As I aged out of my Hinn fascination, I realized that he was full of shit. Though I still think Hinn is full of shit, I love watching him. There is something fascinating about the way Hinn's crusades are all orchestrated and choreographed to bring cures to people. The cures that Hinn sells are not all that different from the cures that are sold in all churches.

My brain doesn't function like a normal brain. Since my childhood, I've realized that my brain was doing things outside of the ordinary. I was well acquainted with mania and depression before I even knew their names. Church drove me crazy. I worried about whether I was saved. I worried about whether I was baptized right. I worried about whether I believed in the resurrection correctly. I worried about whether or not I believed that the Bible was completely true. I knew something was terribly wrong. Worry kept leading to depression and depression kept leading to thoughts of suicide. I couldn't function. Though I've watched the focus of my mania and depression shift and change over the years, one thing has always been constant . . . church drives me crazy.

When I finally made the decision to go to the doctor, I was diagnosed with a Bipolar brain (or Bipolar Disorder). The diagnosis has always made much more sense to me than the Bible. The Bible always wants me to do things. The diagnosis always wants me to be something. After I was diagnosed, I talked to a liberal and conservative preacher about what was going on. They both said the same thing, "Let me pray for God to cure you." I ran out of both offices and have never returned. People who think they need to cure me are very dangerous. They are addicted to normativity in a way that doesn't allow them the room to appreciate the beauty of difference. They are like the Bible and only seem to be able to prescribe one path forward. I don't need all that bullshit. I have the diagnosis and that is enough. The diagnosis is from God. My brain functions exactly as God intends it to function. I don't need no cures. I don't need no Benny Hinns. I don't need to be preached at. I was created in the very image of God. I am perfection in defection. I am enough.

Brains come in billions of different forms. The rush to categorize brains has led to a desire to label anything that is divergent from our conceptions of normal. The problem with such tactics is that those with power and ability are the ones who get to label what is normal. Normal becomes a category of exclusion instead of a category of inclusion. The concept of neurodiversity pushes back against our conclusions of what is normal. Neurodiversity is a belief that various conditions of the human mind are common variations in human development. Basically, neurodiversity is about spreading the belief that people are perfect just the way they are. Neurodivergence is a natural variation that should be celebrated and not condemned with derogatory labels. Cures are not necessary. The neurodivergent were created just the way they are . . . in God's image. The neurodivergent are not alone. God will never fit our normal neurological paradigms. God will eternally be neurodivergent.

"Would you let God cure you?" The question lingered for an extended period of time. I was on a tour promoting my last book and my mental illness came up. After what seemed like an eternity, I raised my head an dproclaimed, "No. I'm perfect just the way that I am. God isn't the cure. God simply is and so am I."

Amen.

JUNE 7, 2016

Stop With the Damn Resolutions

No More Resolutions
Nothing is Ever Resolved
You Are All Still the Cowards You Were
Before You Entered the Voting Halls
Give You Lives to Something More
Than Doing Exactly What You Did Before
These Denominational Votes Are Such A Heist
Be it Resolved to Stop With the Damn Resolutions
And Finally Learn to Live Like Jesus Christ

JUNE 8, 2016

Hillary Clinton is the AntiChrist

*I wrote, "Donald Trump is the AntiChrist" in December 2015 and it is included below.

Here are 5 Reasons I also Think that Hillary Clinton is the AntiChrist:

1. Clinton's immigration policies are opposed to Christ's command to welcome the stranger.

2. Clinton's economic policies are opposed to Christ's command to care for the least of these.

3. Clinton's militaristic outlook on foreign policy is opposed to Christ's command to seek peace.

4. Clinton's policies on race are opposed to Christ's command to love our neighbors as we love ourselves.

5. Clinton's support for the death penalty is opposed to Christ's command to love our enemies.

Our nation now has a choice between two AntiChrists.

Both are different flavors of evil.

What are we to do?

Choose Christ.

Amen.

Donald Trump is the AntiChrist

Fear was a consistent companion. Sleep was elusive. Terror regularly stopped by. The Tribulation Trail was a haunted walk through an interpretation of the Book of Revelation hosted by a church across town. Our annual visit always ushered in months of study and speculation about the end times. During the Trail, there was always a movie projected on a huge sheet that illustrated how close we actually were to the end of the world. Though I tried to convince myself that I didn't believe any of it, I was always shaken to my core. Every year, I regretted that my parents forced me to go. Though I couldn't shake the fear, I committed to erasing all of it from my mind and not believing any of it. In the last few months, I have changed my mind.

From his attacks on Mexicans to his support for roughing up a Black protestor to his calls for a national database for Muslims to his passion for bullying, Donald Trump has provided us no shortage of evidence that he is both a bigot and a racist. Just today, Trump declared his support for barring Muslims from entering the United States. If he weren't so consistently evil, I would think this was some kind of sick joke. Unfortunately, the joke is up. Millions of other racists and bigots have flocked to join forces with him. These are scary days. Back when I was growing up, we were told that the Antichrist would be the opposite of Jesus and gain millions of followers quickly. While I think there are many antichrists who raise their ugly heads throughout history, I have no doubt in this contextual moment that Donald Trump is the chief opposite of Jesus... Donald Trump is the Antichrist.

The great deceiver has convinced millions of people that the best way to love your neighbor is to wall them out, shake them down and put them in their place. This is the opposite of the love of Jesus. The great deceiver has convinced millions that the best way to love your enemies is to bomb them into submission over and over again. This is the opposite of the love of Jesus. The great deceiver has convinced millions that the down and out deserve our contempt rather than our help. This is the opposite of the love Jesus. The great deceiver has convinced millions that bullying is the way to get ahead. This is the opposite of the love of Jesus. The great deceiver has convinced millions that those who are hungry deserve to be hungry. This is the opposite of the love of Jesus. The great deceiver has convinced millions that those who thirst should've thought ahead and prepared better. This is the opposite of the love of Jesus. The great deceiver has convinced millions that the stranger is our enemy. This is the opposite of the love of Jesus. The great deceiver has convinced millions to laugh at those who are without clothes. This is the opposite of the love of Jesus. The great deceiver has convinced millions to work to deny the sickest and poorest amongst us healthcare. This is the opposite of the love of Jesus. The great deceiver has promised to lock up more people. This is the opposite of the love of Jesus. The great deceiver has ridiculed the disabled. This is the opposite of the love of Jesus. The great deceiver is named Donald Trump and is working for the exact opposite of what followers of Jesus should be working for. What has and will be done to those standing in the line of fire of Trump has and will be done to Jesus. Those who stand against Trump at this perilous hour stand against the Antichrist.

Over the last few weeks, I've watched pastors and preachers run to meet and get their picture taken with Trump. These pastors and preachers love their ministries far more than they love the God they claim to serve. In much of the literature about the end of days,

preachers cozy up to evil and forget about Jesus. Looking around at churches, I am seeing this phenomenon happen to more than just leaders. Many years ago, I promised to never look at any of the rapture, tribulation or end of days bullshit I grew up with ever again. I thought it was all so silly and irrelevant to modernity. Now, I look at the evil that is Donald Trump and think twice.
Amen.

JUNE 9, 2016

On Conflict: Conversations with a Disciple

*Christian Parks is accompanying me again this summer. Throughout our time together, we will post brief snippets of our conversations.

C: How should Christians engage conflict?

J: Brother Christian, we are called to create moral conflict. We are called to trouble the waters. We are called to cause a disturbance. I'm not interested in all of these calls for peace when there is no peace. I'm tired of stagnated and decaying Christians telling me to tone it down. In a world of injustice, we need to turn it up. Now, it is often curious what people think turning it up is. All summer, I've been so embarrassed for my colleagues who've worked to get moderate mushy meaningless legislation passed by their moderate mushy meaningless churches. It is hard for me to not see such work as anything more than fearfully avoiding the work that actually must be done. Jesus died for us to now be cowards? Nothing is gained when everything is given away. There is not a damn thing radical about moderation. Our job is to follow the radical of radicals and consistently create moral conflict.

C: I agree Jeff that we must be willing to afflict the comfortable—trouble the waters. What happens when conflict creates hostility that seems to have no end? I know I get tired of fighting. I get tired of being the one who must constantly be at the gates of oppression, yelling and screaming to be heard. What happens when the chaos of the troubled waters becomes overwhelming?

J: I simply cling to Jesus. I know that she won't take me where she can't come get me. I believe that clinging is the greatest spiritual discipline of all.

C: "Clinging" knowing that the road leads to death. Clinging, knowing that rest comes after we have given all that we have. Clinging, knowing that the hope of Christ lies in the queer. Clinging, knowing that clinging is the only thing that has ever changed our world. Clinging.

J: Clinging.

Amen.

JUNE 11, 2016

Learning to Die/Fly

Nearly four years ago, I was working as a chaplain at JPS Hospital in Fort Worth. The downtown level one trauma center was often a wild place to be. On a relatively sleepy Sunday afternoon, we got word that an airplane crash victim from Roanoke was being flown in. I'll never forget what he looked liked when he arrived. I was terrified. I'd never seen a human body look like that before. It was as if someone had crushed him and blown him back up as big as they possibly could him. Pushing against my fear, I moved closer. I'd been on the job for a few weeks. As I searched for life in his eyes, the man looked at me and said, "I'm ok."

Except for the short time at the hospital, I never knew Charlie Yates in life. I only knew him in death. Later, I found out that Yates was a decorated pilot and beloved man. Before anyone told me, I knew that he was a man of deep faith. I could feel it. I saw his faith sustain him in those final moments. While it has been a long time since I worked at JPS, Charlie Yates has stuck with me.

For many years, I've been terrified to fly. I didn't even know that it was possible for a human body to look like that. I tried unsuccessfully to get those images out of my mind. The more I've learned about Yates, the more I've realized that his faith pushed him to face his fear. Last week, I guess I decided I decided to do just that.

Down in Addison, I climbed into a light-sport aircraft for a lesson. I was terrified. As we took off, the plane bounced all over the damn sky. I just knew a wing was about to fall off at any moment. The sweat from my palms accumulated. When we finally arrived at a comfortable cruising altitude, my instructor asked me, "Do you feel comfortable yet?" I replied, "I think it's going to be much longer than the duration of this lesson before my asshole unclinches." Later, I stepped out in faith and took the controls. While flying over North Dallas, I knew I'd conquered my fear. After a harrowing ride down, I finally got back on the ground. Exhilarated, I thought about Charlie Yates. Though I never really knew him, I had a feeling he was there cheering me on.

Amen.

JUNE 12, 2016

Christians are the Real Terrorists

50 people are dead. Orlando's popular nightclub Pulse was supposed to be a place of refuge for the LGBTQ community. Now, it's a crime scene.

There are indications that this was an act of Islamic terrorism. Many will rush to accept this conclusion and direct their anger towards Muslims. I know better. No matter what the motive of this particular shooter was, I know who is most responsible for the repeated terror that afflicts the LGBTQ community in this country.

Christians are the real terrorists. From direct violence to reparative therapies to continued debates about full inclusion, Christians belong in the same category as these Islamic terrorists. The only difference is that Christians have been more prolific. Christians can claim millions upon millions of LGBTQ victims.

Jesus is embodied in the marginalized and oppressed.

The LGBTQ community faces Christian marginalization and oppression everyday.

How can anyone follow Jesus without the LGBTQ community?

Today is the day of salvation.

Amen.

JUNE 13, 2016

Move Your Ass

Move Your Ass
Get Out of Your Seat
We Have Got to Pray for These Streets

Don't Delay
We Haven't the Time
To Sit Around and Wait for the Next Crime

Move Your Ass
Get Out of Your Seats
We Have Got to Pray for These Streets

Keep Walking
Mind Every Crack
We Haven't the Time
To Sit Around and Wait for the Next Attack

Move Your Ass
Get Out of Your Seats
We Have Got to Pray for These Streets

Amen.

JUNE 14, 2016

On Tomorrow: Conversations with a Disciple

*Christian Parks is accompanying me again this summer. Throughout our time together, we will post brief snippets of our conversations.

J: How do you move forward?

C: I pass through lament and anger. I look injustice and hatred in the eye and declare there is another way. I look into myself and look into our world and proclaim there is a higher calling—a greater calling. I walk forward never forgetting what darkness can do, so I seek light. I seek a light beyond the world we have created. Orlando isn't the first and sadly won't be the last. I push toward hope. Then again, what is hope?

J: Hope is a direction. Love is the destination. Hope is love becoming flesh. There is no hope apart from such a love.

C: May we place our hope in a fleshy kind of love.

J: Though hope has been stretched, we will not despair. I trust the author and source of hope to guide our way.

Amen.

JUNE 17, 2016

On the One Year Anniversary of the Tragedy at Mother Emanuel AME Church

Almost a year ago, I released this statement to numerous outlets after learning of the shooting at Mother Emanuel Church:

"Tragedy amplifies our desperate desire to hear a word from God. In the midst of suffocating times, sojourners gathered last night and placed their ears to the sky. As a testament to their love, the group welcomed a stranger. When the shots rang out, the nine souls of Mother Emanuel AME Church heard the beautiful comforting of words of God, 'Let not your hearts be troubled . . . ' As we hear the echoes of last night, may we not forget that God is preparing a place for us beyond all that holds us back. If we are willing, racism and violence can die today. Listen. Can you hear the words of God calling us to make it so?"

Today, I believe these words as much as I ever have.

Amen.

JUNE 18, 2016

On the 10th Anniversary of My Ordination

Jesus called me into ministry.

The institutional church has put me through hell.

The keepers of the normative have always tried to stand in my way.

Having spent years in discernment, I will never forget the first question. "Do you believe in a literal hell?" After an afternoon of similar questions, I passed my ordination council. When the service started, I sat in the front. Dozens of men placed their hands on my head. At the end, my dearest mentor stood up and declared me "a strange man ordained to a strange ministry for a strange world."

Ten years after my ordination, Jesus is still calling me.

The institutional church still tries to block my work.

The marginalized and oppressed always guide me through.

Just this past week, I felt the hands again. One by one, the children of God at the Church at the Table in Fort Worth stopped to affirm and celebrate my ministry. In the midst of the reverence of it all, Jesus showed up. One of my dear friends shouted out, "Keep blowing shit up baby!"

The Violence of Being

I will.

Amen.

JUNE 18, 2016

The Beyond Stunning Hypocrisy of the Cooperative Baptist Fellowship

The Cooperative Baptist Fellowship responded swiftly to the recent crises in Orlando. From pastoral care to providing care packages to a variety of other services, churches and individuals affiliated with the Cooperative Baptist Fellowship really stepped up. These actions should be commended.

Unfortunately, the care and services provided are not the entirety of the story. For every LGBTQ person the Cooperative Baptist Fellowship touched this last week, we know there is at least one thing they didn't hear, "You're hired." While Cooperative Baptist Fellowship leaders expressed their grief about the dozens who died, they didn't admit that they would've discriminated against them in life. The Cooperative Baptist Fellowship maintains blatantly hateful homophobic policies.

As Baptist Christians, we believe that the foundation of a Christian sexual ethic is faithfulness in marriage between a man and a woman and celibacy in singleness. We also believe in the love and grace of God for all people, both for those who live by this understanding of the biblical standard and those who do not. We treasure the freedom of individual conscience and the autonomy of the local church, and we also believe that congregational leaders should be persons of moral integrity whose lives exemplify the highest standards of Christian conduct and character.

Because of this organizational value, the Cooperative Baptist Fellowship does not allow for the expenditure of funds for organizations or causes that condone, advocate or affirm homosexual practice. Neither does this CBF organizational value allow for the purposeful hiring of a staff person or the sending of a missionary who is a practicing homosexual.

-Adopted by the Coordinating Council of the Cooperative Baptist Fellowship, October 2000

The hypocrisy is beyond stunning. As the Cooperative Baptist Fellowship meets in Greensboro, North Carolina next week, let's pray that they save themselves from their hateful homophobia.

Amen.

JUNE 20, 2016

The Gospel Next Door

Where are we going? How did we get here? What does tomorrow hold?

God is making all things new.

Don't believe it?

Walk next door.

I get turned around on the journey. I get confused. I lose my sense of direction. I get afraid. I feel like I should give up.

I need Jesus.

I need next door.

Marty Troyer's *The Gospel Next Door* is a helpful and timely reminder that next door is always right next door.

Amen.

JUNE 20, 2016

We're Dead: Guns Mattered More

With the defeat of multiple gun control measures this evening, the US Senate has made it clear that they believe that guns matter more than human lives.

The blood that flowed out of Mother Emanuel AME Church doesn't matter.

The blood that flowed out of Pulse Nightclub doesn't matter.

The blood that flowed out of Sandy Hook Elementary doesn't matter.

The blood that flows down our streets day in and day out doesn't matter.

Only guns matter in America.

Shots fired.

Jesus has been hit.

Pack it up.

The game is up.

We're Dead: Guns Mattered More

We're dead.

Guns mattered more.

And Jesus is bleeding out in the street.

Amen.

JUNE 24, 2016

Dialogues with a Disciple: On the Ocean

C: In a break from visiting with the guys on death row, we had an amazing opportunity to witness the last glimpse of the Strawberry Moon over the ocean in Galveston. What did God say?

J: The pull of the ocean is always strong. There is something about the movement of those waves. The moon leads the dancing. A multitude of witnesses gather for the performance of the Divine. The ocean always makes me feel like I'm a part of the performance. God told me to move. What did God say to you?

C: In the midst of turbulent transition, God said "don't afraid, my child. Just as a dance with the moon as it dances with the waves, so do I dance with you. Trust your steps. You may crash into the rocks with great force, know it is all part of the process—your process."

J: It's amazing that every grain of sand is a refraction of a boundlessly loving God. As I walked on the beach, I felt the presence of the ancestors, the now-cestors, and the future-cestors. The cestors presence reminds me that I'm not alone in the pursuit of a queer reality that refracts our queer eternity.

C: May we never forget that we're not alone.

Amen.

JUNE 25, 2016

The Cost of Your Plate

Would you eat beef that cost a forest?

Would you eat fish that cost an ocean?

Would you eat meat that cost starvation?

Where are you going to put all of these animals?

How are you going to stop global warming when your diet causes it?

The questions of destruction are endless.

The cost of your plate is greater than you could ever imagine.

You have to learn to eat for each other.

There is one food that is destroying our land, sea and skies.

Meat.

Can you stop?

Will you put down the knife?

Let's learn to love again.

Amen.

JUNE 26, 2016

The Passion of Charles Moore: Two Years Later

The Rev. Charles Moore visits me often. For over two years now, I've closed my eyes and felt the pull of his flame. The media attention is over. Too much time has passed for most. Our memories are so frail. I won't ever be able to forget. I still see the flames. To commemorate the passion, I've decided to repost on the blog that I wrote after hearing about Moore's self-immolation. I encourage you to sit for a moment with the martyr of Grand Saline:

Don't You Dare Turn Your Head: The Self-Immolation of The Rev. Charles Moore

The fiery passion of 79-year-old retired United Methodist pastor The Rev. Charles Moore is raging in my soul right now. On June 23 around 5:30pm, Moore exited his vehicle in Grand Saline, Texas, doused his body with gasoline and set himself on fire. After rescue efforts by bystanders, Moore was taken by helicopter to Parkland Hospital in Dallas and eventually died late last night. Based on notes left behind, Moore chose to self-immolate based on his frustration with the United Methodist Church's position on human sexuality, opposition to the death penalty, disdain for racism (especially in his hometown of Grand Saline) and his deep anger at Southern Methodist University's decision to house the George W. Bush Presidential Center.

The Passion of Charles Moore: Two Years Later

Rev. Moore knew how we would react. On June 22, the day before he self-immolated, Moore wrote, "I know that some will judge me insane." When I first shared Moore's story with a table full of people at a Dallas restaurant, everyone immediately declared him insane. I know different.

While a graduate student in history at the University of Alabama, I spent six months studying self-immolations that took place in both the United States and in Vietnam during the Vietnam War. With stark consistency, the persons who self-immolated that I studied were remarkably sane and unquestionably persons of deep conviction. The temptation of the hour will be to turn our heads and call The Rev. Charles Moore insane. If we do . . . we should also turn our heads from Jesus and call him insane too. For we must not forget, Jesus sat in the Garden of Gethsemane and made a conscious clear decision to step out into death . . . just like Moore.

Instead of judging Rev. Moore, maybe we should try to ignite the passion for justice that burned so brightly in his life in ours. When Texas tries to execute Manuel Vasquez on August 6, maybe we should do something more than simply turn our heads and protect our dignity. When our churches and societies ignore racial segregation and discrimination, maybe we should do something more than simply turn our heads and protect our pride. When we are asked to perform a same-sex wedding ceremony or ordain a same-gender loving person, maybe we should do something more than turn our heads and protect our salaries/pensions. When institutional injustices occur all around us, maybe we should do something more that turn our heads and bless them with our silence. I will go to bed this evening thankful for the public witness of The Rev. Charles Moore and pray that the church would garner even an ounce of his passion and courage.

On a personal note, I serve on the Board of Directors of the Texas Coalition to Abolish the Death Penalty. Rev. Moore helped found the organization. Because Moore lived, I am able to do the work that I do. My respect for Moore is unwavering and I am proud to follow in his footsteps. Jesus asks us to give our lives and Moore did.

Tonight my passion for Jesus burns as intensely as ever. When I look straight ahead into the dark, I see Moore's bespectacled image burning. I see Moore giving his life so that others might live. I refuse to turn my head. I know that Jesus is speaking to me from there. The courage of a passionate follower of Jesus can set the world afire with love. May the great martyrdom of The Rev. Charles Moore make it so.

Amen.

details from:
http://www.umc.org/news-and-media/retired-pastor-saw-destiny-in-self-immolation

JUNE 27, 2016

The Tall Grass

The Tall Grass
Neighbor to the Water
Creates a Hole
Beauty Grows
The Greens
The Blues
Remind Me of You
North Dakota
Driving Well
Fighting Back
Against All Hell
We Roll On
We Can't Stop
It's Seabeck, Washington
Or Drop
The Tall Grass
Moving
Shaking
Shifting
Growing
Tell Me All of Your Secrets
Calling
Wooing
Pulling
How Can I Trust You?
How Can I trust Anyone?

The Violence of Being

The Tall Grass
Bows Down
Singing Praises
To The Deep
The Waves
Drop and Rise
Chasing Tomorrow
That Place Beyond Our Eyes
But What About Today?
The Tall Grass
Offers No Advice
The Tall Grass Simply Is
Is is Enough

JUNE 29, 2016

Cracked Eyes

Cracked Eyes
I've Traveled Far
Today Grows Longer
And Longer
Cracked Eyes
I've Traveled Far
Where Are We Going
Are We Near
Cracked Eyes
I Need You to Close

Heat

My Thoughts Betray My Reality
Where Were You When Sweat Poured Down My Neck
The Elusive Cold
I Trusted You
Now, I'm Back to Sweat
Lying on these Leather Seats
Dreaming of You
Yearning for Your Coolness
I Sweat

The Set

Light Retreats

The Violence of Being

How Did We Even Meet
You Called to Me
How Did You Know My Name
I'd Never Heard it Before
I Strain to Hear it Again
The Sun is Gone

JUNE 30, 2016

United Methodist Insensitivity Unleashed in North Texas

"What were they thinking?"

I almost didn't write this piece. People kept telling me how nice the people in the photograph are. I don't doubt it. One question remains.

"What were they thinking?"

Pictured are 5 United Methodist ministers in the North Texas Annual Conference. The picture was taken at a United Methodist camp dedicated to educating the next generation. One question remains.

"What were they thinking?"

This photograph is disturbing. A United Methodist minister is pointing her fingers in the shape of a gun directly at the camera. The United Methodist ministers all have mug shots on their shirts. The United Methodist ministers are all posing in various ways seeking to mimic hip-hop culture. I could go on and on. The bottom line is that this photograph intentionally seeks to make a mockery of the experiences of black people. One question remains.

The Violence of Being

"What were they thinking?"

The photograph is racist. The insensitivity that it takes to take a picture like this is beyond egregious. I can't believe that the North Texas Annual Conference of the United Methodist Church hasn't done more about it. I'm sure the continued segregation amongst their churches plays a role in the subdued response. Regardless, these folks need cultural sensitivity training immediately. There will be many who disagree. There will be many who wish that I hadn't shared this picture. They will be the reason we keep seeing racist pictures like this.

Amen.

JULY 2, 2016

Spiritual Discipline is Spiritual Destruction

God is never more distant than when talk of spiritual disciplines arises.

Darkness touched every crevice of the room. We had come to have an experience with God. This was our weekend. Spiritual discipline weekends were common in the world I grew up in. I never wanted to go. I never felt like anything was real. Then, things popped off. Light flooded the stage. The music pounded. I could feel my organs jiggling around inside my body. Ricky Rufio ran on stage pumping his fists. As all attention focused on Rufio, the entire room started to chant repeatedly, "Jesus! Jesus! Jesus! Jesus! Jesus! Jesus!" I can still hear it. Before Rufio started talking, we flailed our hands wildly in praise. Rufio pointed directly at us and declared, "You need a standing appoint me with God." For just under an hour, we were pounded with ideas of spiritual discipline. Then, the music kicked back up. As the guitar chords cycled repeatedly in our ears, we were called to the front. "If you want to commit to a standing appointment, run down to this altar and declare it to God." I did. We all did. We wanted a closer relationship. We felt like we needed it. The night began a period of searching for me. After keeping a quiet time of prayer, scripture meditation and solitude for a few weeks, I knew that shit wasn't for me. Scripture meditation reminded me of why I didn't read the Bible more often. Solitude only made me feel lonely. Quiet only made God more absent. I walked away from it all.

The Violence of Being

Spiritual discipline is spiritual destruction.

Different theologies offer different paths. Whatever I had wasn't working, so I decided to try a new path. "Beat your mind into submission." I remember my spiritual mentor repeatedly telling me that I needed discipline. The words always felt so violent. I assumed that they were the words of God. For a number of years, I tried hard. I fasted on a regular basis. The only thing I experienced was hunger. I practiced rest. I just got bored. I tried stillness. I almost lost my mind. Eventually, I realized that none of this was about God.

There is nothing organic about spiritual discipline.

I walked into the room. Candles were everywhere. The spiritual retreat was the first time I'd tried anything dealing with spiritual disciplines in a very long time. The leader of the gathering walked in. For about an hour, she hummed. I couldn't figure out when she was going to stop. When she did, she said, "In order to listen to God, we're going to be silent the rest of the weekend." I knew that I was done. Slowly, I stood up and started to make my way toward the door. Before I could get out unnoticed, the leader of the spiritual retreat looked up and questioned,

"Where are you going?" I replied, "Silence doesn't work for me. I just don't do well with silence." In fear that her entire retreat was going to fall apart, the woman snapped back, "Those who don't do silence ... don't do God." I knew that was it. I left and never looked back.

Spiritual discipline has always been forced. God is not forced. God simply is.

Spirituality is about pressing into the "isness" of God. We are the "isness" God. We are made in God's image. We are spiritual. We are enough. We don't need more discipline. We need more being.

Spiritual Discipline is Spiritual Destruction

There are twelve spiritual practices I think would be helpful to our beings.

Movement is about refusing to be still.

Noise is about refusing to be silent.

Engagement is about to refusing to give in to the temptation of solitude.

Eating is about eating correctly and refusing to fast.

Being is about refusing to pray.

Deconstruction is about pushing back against the idea of meditating.

Immolation is about setting the person on fire within for life celebration and refusing to be caught up in external worship.

Risk is about refusing to be chained to ideas of trust.

Pain is about realizing that complete wellness is not possible.

Becoming is refusing to stay where you are.

Action is about rejecting ideas of rest.

Pushing is about exercising spiritual force to transform the world.

God is about movement. Our spiritual disciplines have long given us reason to stop when we should have been moving. Spirituality can be so much more than it currently is. Spirituality can transform the world.

Amen.

JULY 4, 2016

The Day After the 4th

The Cost of Patriotism

Born of Fear
Scared as Hell
Salvation Decisions
Full Jails
We Invaded
Millions Die
Red, White and Blue
Apple Pie
The World Starves
Choirs Sing
We Destroyed Everything
We Matter
We Alone
We Don't Care
About Your Home
The Flood of Blood
Took Our Brain
The Pain of Arrogance
Did the Same
No More Blessings
No More Dreams
God was Never
On Our Team
Our Only Hope

The Day After the 4th

Is to Step Back
And Finally Cease the Attack
Ultimately,
God will be Found
Starving to Death
Right Downtown
Until Then,
We'll Never Win
We'll Just Sit
Drowning in American Shit

JULY 16, 2016

Now

To Be Visible
To Be Invisible
To Be
To Be Human
To Not
To Be
To Rot
To Know
To Pray
To Go
To Think
To Strive
To Dream
To Be
The Future Forgot Us
We're Stuck Here
We Know There's More
We Just Don't Know What It's For

JULY 18, 2016

Babel.

Writing used to be easy. Now, nothing seems easy. Leaning in, I just stare at the screen. Occasionally, I try to type something. Despite my desperation to write, my mind is held captive to a former place.

Bloody films never leave you. Every image sticks. The officer took his gun and shot Alton Sterling dead. Amidst the screams, Philando Castile bled out. Everyone wanted to talk about their lives, I couldn't get past their deaths. I wasn't alone. We put out a call. Over a thousand people responded.

Downtown Dallas has been the site of dozens and dozens of rallies. Over the last year, we've repeatedly marched for endangered lives. The rally was large. We didn't hesitate. The crowd was ready to go. The speakers were ready to go. We were ready to go. Cries of justice rang out.

In the midst of misery, God is incarnate. When we believe all is lost, God speaks from the bones. The bones rise up and lead us on. They did that night.

I was nervous about speaking. When I opened my mouth, everything seemed clear. Though I spoke for a long time, people have only remembered one phrase, "God Damn White America." The gathered understood the adaptation of Jeremiah Wright's infamous phrasing. The message of unity was simple. The message of love was heard. We must become one. There is no White America. There is only America. Violence has a way of creating confusion.

Fear is not a part of faith. I didn't care. I was afraid.

Safety was at the front of my mind. The Dallas Police Department guided the marchers through downtown with tremendous grace. On multiple occasions, we stopped or changed routes to make sure that everyone had the chance to keep up. I stayed at the front of the line. In time, I settled into the rhythm of the movement. Throughout the march, anything seemed possible. Love and justice was within our grasp. Then, confusion reigned.

Darkness was all Jesus knew. The disciples professed their allegiance to him. Now, they couldn't even stay awake. Unable to function, Jesus cried out in fear. No one was woke.

Our march wound through downtown. Stopping at the Old Courthouse, we took a minute to talk about the 1910 lynching of Allen Brooks. There was no denying that the march for love and justice was long. For a few seconds, I stared at the bricks.

What did they know? What would they say? How much further is the journey? Organizers and the police shouted for me to run up to the front of the march. I did.

For the next few blocks, I talked to a DPD Major. In the midst of the rally and protest winding down, we talked about the success of the night. The conversation felt natural. There seemed to be a genuine connection. A few steps past Austin St., everything changed.

Things seemed clearer before Babel. Now, no one speaks the same language. Confusion is all anyone knows.

"Pop-pop-pop-pop-pop . . . " I heard it so clearly. I've heard it ever since. The shots rang out. The violence was all that was clear. Bullets flew in every direction. Multiple people dropped. The echoes only enhanced the terror of it all. Pandemonium took over. Grabbing my shirt to make sure I hadn't been shot, I ran back toward the protestors. I was terrified that a thousand people were about to walk into the middle of a shootout. Throughout the evening, I carried a 10-foot cross. At this moment, I used it as a shepherd's staff and started swinging it around. Screaming, "Run! Run! Active Shooter! Active Shooter! Go! Go!" I got as many people out of there as I could.

The march was beautiful. Every step was about stopping violence. Love and justice seemed so loud and so close. Evil didn't listen. 5 Officers were Dead. Devastation set in.

Total confusion arrived.

For the next few days, I told my story on every major news outlet in the country and beyond. The officers were never far from my mind. Repeatedly, I reminded people that this was a nonviolent peaceful protest. "Love" and "justice" were the only words on my lips. I looked directly into the camera and declared, "Stop shooting America!" I don't know if anyone heard me. Violence always confuses the ears. I saw it happen. I saw it happen again in Baton Rouge. Former words are confused and present words are confusing. We will not be able to understand until we stand down.

Oh God, deliver us from Babel.

Amen.

JULY 20, 2016

City Council.

These are difficult times. As many of you know, I have given my life to the struggle for social justice. Almost two weeks ago, my life changed. I organized a peaceful rally calling for an end to police brutality. Before the night was over, 5 officers were dead. Though it was beyond apparent that the shooter acted alone, I became the object of intense scrutiny and fabrications from the nether regions of the media. Death threats started to pour in by the hundreds. There was no question that we weren't equipped to deal with what we were facing. After realizing we needed outside help, we reached out to Councilwoman Keely Briggs. Not long after, Chief Lee Howell contacted me.

I realize that I'm an unlikely source to praise the Denton Police Department. Over the last few years, I have spent much time criticizing police departments throughout our country. Regardless, Chief Howell and his department protected us at a perilous hour. Officer after officer came by the house and sat outside to make sure that we were ok. Even though my face was all over television, no one showed anger about my actions. Everyone just offered empathy and compassion. I am unbelievably thankful. Chief Howell and his department showed that they were professionals above all else.

Though I'm sure there will come a time in which we disagree again, I will be forever grateful for the actions that Chief Howell and his department took over the last few weeks. Together, we stared down terror and won.

Rev. Dr. Jeff Hood

JULY 24, 2016

Future

God is Dead
That's exactly what I said
I feel so alone
No one is home
Why do I pray
To waste the day
Why can't I just be
Stay awake with me
How will this stop
Shots falling
Bodies dropping
Blood splattering
Daddy don't get shot
Out of the mouth of the children
The cries rise
I hear it in your eyes
If God's not a joke
Better stay woke

JULY 26, 2016

The Passion of Jacques Hamel

Early this morning, terrorists stormed a church in Normandy, France. When the doors flew open, an 86-year-old priest named Jascques Hamel was standing down front performing Mass. Before much resistance could be mustered, the terrorists cut the throat of Hamel and took several others hostage. Over an extended period of time, Hamel bled out and died.

Throughout the years, Hamel had pledged to serve the church "until *his* last breath." In a world of chaos, may all followers of Jesus exercise such devotion. If violence comes for us, may we have the courage to follow Hamel and bleed out for Christ.

So that we will know the way, let the image of Jascques Hamel never be far from our eyes.

Amen.

JULY 29, 2016

The Absence of Peace

God is a failed concept.

Peace has left us.

We are amongst the forgotten.

Everyone wanted to talk a few weeks ago.

Now, other horrors have garnered the attention of our nation.

We are alone again.

Writing used to be easy. Now, nothing seems easy. Leaning in, I just stare at the screen. Occasionally, I try to type something. Every key gets heavier. How do you describe the indescribable? Despite my desperation to write, my mind is held captive to a former place.

Bloody films never leave you. Every image sticks. The officer took his gun and shot Alton Sterling dead. Amidst the screams, Philando Castile bled out. Everyone wanted to talk about their lives, I couldn't get past their deaths. I wasn't alone. We put out a call. Over a thousand people responded.

Downtown Dallas has been the site of dozens and dozens of rallies. Over the last year, we've repeatedly marched for endangered lives. The rally was large. We didn't hesitate. The crowd was ready to go.

The Violence of Being

The speakers were ready to go. We were ready to go. Cries of justice rang out.

In the midst of misery, God is incarnate. When we believe all is lost, God speaks from the bones. The bones rise up and lead us on. They did that night.

I was nervous about speaking. When I opened my mouth, everything seemed clear. Though I spoke for a long time, people have only remembered one phrase, "God Damn White America." The gathered understood the adaptation of Jeremiah Wright's infamous phrasing. The message of unity was simple. The message of love was heard. We must become one. There is no White America. There is only America. Violence has a way of creating confusion.

Fear is not a part of faith. I didn't care. I was afraid.

Safety was at the front of my mind. The Dallas Police Department guided the marchers through downtown with tremendous grace. On multiple occasions, we stopped or changed routes to make sure that everyone had the chance to keep up. I stayed at the front of the line. In time, I settled into the rhythm of the movement. Throughout the march, anything seemed possible. Love and justice was within our grasp. Then, confusion reigned.

Darkness was all Jesus knew. The disciples professed their allegiance to him. Now, they couldn't even stay awake. Unable to function, Jesus cried out in fear. No one was woke.

Our march wound through downtown. Stopping at the Old Courthouse, we took a minute to talk about the 1910 lynching of Allen Brooks. There was no denying that the march for love and justice was long. For a few seconds, I stared at the bricks. What did they know? What would they say? How much further is the journey? Organizers and the police shouted for me to run up to the front of the march. I did.

The Absence of Peace

For the next few blocks, I talked to a DPD Major. In the midst of the rally and protest winding down, we talked about the success of the night. The conversation felt natural. There seemed to be a genuine connection. A few steps past Austin St., everything changed.

Things seemed clearer before Babel. Now, no one speaks the same language. Confusion is all anyone knows.

"Pop-pop-pop-pop-pop . . . " I heard it so clearly. I've heard it ever since. The shots rang out. The violence was all that was clear. Bullets flew in every direction. Multiple people dropped. The echoes only enhanced the terror of it all. Pandemonium took over. Grabbing my shirt to make sure I hadn't been shot, I ran back toward the protestors. I was terrified that a thousand people were about to walk into the middle of a shootout. Throughout the evening, I carried a 10-foot cross. At this moment, I used it as a shepherd's staff and started swinging it around. Screaming, "Run! Run! Active Shooter! Active Shooter! Go! Go!" I got as many people out of there as I could.

The march was beautiful. Every step was about stopping violence. Love and justice seemed so loud and so close. Evil didn't listen. 5 Officers were Dead. Devastation set in.

Total confusion arrived.

For the next few days, I told my story on every major news outlet in the country and beyond. The officers were never far from my mind. Repeatedly, I reminded people that this was a nonviolent peaceful protest. "Love" and "justice" were the only words on my lips. I looked directly into the camera and declared, "Stop shooting America!" I don't know if anyone heard me. Violence always confuses the ears.

The Violence of Being

I saw it happen. I saw it happen again in Baton Rouge. Former words are confused and present words are confusing. We will not be able to understand until we stand down.

Stop!

Threats collect. Death seems near. Police protection never seemed like something I would ever want or need. My children mean so much to me. Should they play outside? "Daddy, what's going on?" Pain is a dull instrument that keeps plunging into my soul. How could all of this happen? I have to figure it out. I have to know. I have to stop this from happening again. I have to think. I can't hear. The words are difficult understand. There are so many words. There is so much Babel.

I have to concentrate on the few voices that I can trust.

Don't invite me to church. God died. God died when those police officers dropped. God died when the victims of police brutality dropped. How can you keep talking about God when we know that God is dead? We saw God shot. We saw God bleed out. We saw God transported to the hospital. We know God left us. We have mourned God. The only thing I have to say to God right now is, "Give us something worth believing in!"

I want to believe.

I'm trying.

Oh God, deliver us from Babel.

Maybe, there is peace out there.

Amen.

JULY 30, 2016

Don't Go To Church.
Be The Church.

Shortly before being arrested for civil disobedience, I said these words at the Dallas Rally Against Police Brutality in December of 2014:

There is an indictment against our religious communities. That indictment is here tonight. Asking the question . . . How long? How long must we work? How long must we wait for justice? How long will you sit in your religious buildings and castles and do nothing? I have thought about what the church is over the past few weeks. I have decided that the buildings and the spaces don't matter. I have decided that the crosses and other religious paraphernalia are but mirages. I believe that the Spirit of God is not contained in such things. I believe that the spirit of God is right here tonight. I believe that the true church *is here*.

Don't Go To Church. Be The Church.

Amen.

AUGUST 4, 2016

Relearning to Think: Thoughts from Dallas

The world was in chaos.

"God Damn White America." I don't know that I've uttered words that have been more misunderstood. I don't know that I have uttered words that have been more understood. I stood before a huge crowd. There were only seconds to go before it was time for me to speak. The words bubbled up is such a way that I knew where they were from. It has always seemed clear to me that any idea of America that excludes anyone deserves to be damned.

Feet were constantly hitting the pavement. Victims of police brutality filled the minds of the gathered. Hundreds and hundreds of souls yearning for justice marched down the glowing streets of Dallas. Energy was high. I could feel it in my bones. Whispers of hope filled the air. The diners stood in reverence. Nobody was able to avert their eyes. Endurance mingled with the heat. Sweat dropped to the pavement. There was no stopping us. We wanted justice. God was there somewhere.

Old bricks pulled us forward. Centuries of injustice drew us together. The Historic Dallas County Courthouse is a mound of red rock cascading to the sky. The back steps were a fitting place to remember. The screams for blood grew louder and louder. After fighting their way into the courthouse, several thousand people

Relearning to Think: Thoughts from Dallas

drug Allen Brooks out of his trial. Not long after, the mob lynched Brooks. Throughout the day, Brooks body was on display. Postcards were created to commemorate the event. Though it happened in 1910, my brain felt like it was closer than I could have ever dreamed. The hanging. The dragging. The hating. "Jeff!" I snapped out of it. I had to lead everyone back to where we started. Running up front, I took my position at the front with the large cross that I'd carried most of the night. After a few moments, we started walking.

The chants had subsided. Everyone just seemed to be humming. Divine buzz surrounded us. The Major and I chatted about how positive the night had been. Everything seemed to be fine. Though I was still in strong spirits, I was very tired. Any event of this size or magnitude really takes the wind out of the organizers. My brain seemed to be slowing down in anticipation of the end of the protest. Shots. Time stopped.

Ringing. Ringing. Ringing. I'd never heard a noise so consistent. In the distance, I saw multiple people drop to the ground. Shots. It took me another second to figure out what was going on. When I realized that someone was shooting, I stared into the distance. Shots. I picked up my cross and swung around. Echoes surrounded me. I didn't know where the shots were coming from. I didn't know who was going to be next. I just knew that there were hundreds of people behind me that were potential victims. Lowering my cross to a staff, I ran to get as many people out of there as I could. Parts of my brain are still on Commerce St.

Cameras were everywhere. Everyone wanted to talk. From early in the morning until late at night, I did interviews in the scorching heat. Flashbacks of the night before kept running through my brain. Shots. Terror. Desperation. The images cycled around and around. It wasn't like watching a movie. It hasn't been since. The images are more like a kaleidoscope. The colors are slightly distorted and repeatedly cycling. My brain just won't snap out of it. Throughout the day, I recalled everything I knew. Even when I didn't want to remember, I forced my brain to work. It was important that the world knew that we held a nonviolent protest that was sabotaged. Though I had no problem telling the details of what I experienced, I still couldn't figure out how it happened. I just wanted to talk about love and justice. How did these officers get killed? Though the world demanded more and more details, I needed to grab hold of my brain. I was tired. I was devastated. I was on. "Rev. Hood, what happened last night?"

Time sped up. The threats were endless. Life seemed to blur. Death lurked behind every door. The phone continued to ring incessantly with interview requests. My brain wasn't working. Thoughts wouldn't form. Talking seemed difficult. I started to receive police protection. Our five children under the age of four were not fooled. Consistently, our children demanded answers. I demanded answers of myself. I couldn't figure out how these officers were dead. There was no amount of exercises or counseling that could get my brain thinking correctly. It didn't matter. I had a sermon to preach. "We are called to give our bodies to the struggle against injustice."

Weeks passed. Trauma grew. I still hear the gunshots. I still feel the terror. I still see the faces of the fallen. Slowly, I am relearning to think. It's almost like I have to catch my thoughts and wrestle them to the ground. Even though it's difficult, I haven't stopped thinking. I know the world needs thinkers right now. Just last Sunday, I was reminded why I still work to think.

Before I could get out the door, my young son said, "Please Daddy, Don't get shot in Dallas."

The shots.

The world is still in chaos.

Amen.

AUGUST 18, 2016

Curbing Our Free Speech

Milwaukee is in flames. Though the name of the city has changed, the recipe for chaos is the same.

Shots are fired. Bullets ignite the anger of oppressed peoples. Officials rush to the nearest camera to express disbelief. The pain of the community is on full display. Everyone calls for discourse.

The problem is that no one can imagine a future different from the past. Ultimately, the chaos becomes manageable. Speech that arises from the flames is squashed. In a time of forced unity, dissent is simply too costly.

Already, just a month removed from the July 7 police ambush, we see it in Dallas.

But first, let's go back even further, to a different Dallas rally, in June. After 49 people were killed at the Pulse nightclub shooting, hundreds gathered here for the Orlando to Dallas Vigil and March. Beautiful words filled the air. Rain gently fell. People seemed united in their desire to end the hate. By the time the march started, I saw numerous law enforcement officials I knew—and one I'd never met before.

For a second, I hesitated. As an outspoken critic of police brutality, I'd spoken very harshly of the Dallas Police Department. Despite the unity at the event, I still believed all my criticisms. Regardless,

I needed to take a chance on loving my neighbor. Turning around, I said: "Chief Brown. I'm Jeff Hood."

Chief David Brown and I marched down the street together and talked. With every step, we exchanged life. We talked about my dad serving as fire chief of two metropolitan departments. The Chief talked about his pride in being part of the march. Before the conversation ended, I was surprised that I'd grown to like Brown. Strengthened in hope, I prayed the Chief would be the one to end police brutality in Dallas.

As the month passed, the world seemed to grow only more frightening. Police brutality was on the rise. Anger was growing. I helped organize a march on July 7 to provide people a chance to respond. The rhetoric was hot. I was particularly incensed. Black and brown bodies were pilling up by the hour. Throughout the event, the Dallas Police Department protected our civil liberties. I worked with an officer the entire time. Toward the end of the march, the officer and I were talking about how peaceful the event was when the shots went off. Immediately, the officers sprang into action. Chaos ensued. When the smoke dissipated, it became clear that Brent Thompson, Patrick Zamarripa, Michael Krol, Lorne Ahrens and Michael Smith died protecting our civil liberties.

The next day, Chief Brown noted: "Police officers are guardians of this great democracy; the freedom to protest, the freedom of speech, freedom of expression. All freedoms we fight for—with our lives." On this, Brown and I are in complete agreement.

Since the shooting, I've committed myself to honoring the sacrifices of the fallen officers by continuing to exercise my civil liberties. I encourage the community to do the same.

I'd thought Brown and I were on the same page, so I was surprised to hear last week that the chief was negotiating with activists to give up their civil liberties in order to secure a meeting with him.

Curbing Our Free Speech

He demanded that they call off a planned protest. "What's more important than our officers' safety. . . . Cancel it and don't schedule anymore in the downtown area. . . . I insist," Brown wrote. As the precondition of a meeting with a public official, these words should frighten anyone who values living in a free society. I'm still praying the Chief simply misspoke.

In this community, our civil liberties have been bought with blood. None of us who survived the July 7 shooting did so only to have those liberties exchanged for a meeting. The cost of freedom is too high for such a concession.

Amid the dangers of our world, let's take the opportunity to open our doors and meet with each other. Let us put aside differences and dialogue, as Chief Brown and I did when we first met. Then, let us march forward together in the unity of justice. Is progress not what our civil liberties are for?

AUGUST 19, 2016

Jeff Wood Letter

*Right before Jeff Wood was given a stay.

To the Editor.

There's an injustice going on.

Jeff Wood didn't kill anyone.

During the robbery of a convenience store in Kerrville, Texas, Wood was the driver of a getaway car. Daniel Reneau is the one who actually robbed the store and killed the clerk, Kriss Kerran. Much evidence has been presented that Wood didn't even know that Renau planned to rob the place or that a gun was involved. Even prosecutors admit that Wood didn't kill anyone. Despite these certainties, prosecutors were able to secure a death sentence based on Texas' infamous Law of Parties. The law is used to prosecute people who are party to a murder. The law hinges on the accused party having reasonable knowledge that a murder is being committed. Questions remain of just how much knowledge Wood had. The case remains quite fuzzy.

Texas plans to execute Wood on August 24.

For Christians, this is an easy case to respond to.

We are called to love our neighbors.

Jeff Wood Letter

How can we love Mr. Wood and kill him?

We can't.

The Rev. Dr. Jeff Hood
Abolitionist,
Denton, Texas

AUGUST 31, 2016

The Sunday Existentialist

Eyes wired shut. Repeated rapid pupil movements. Face up. Head toward the ceiling. Nostrils sucking in air. Chest at ease. Arms relaxed. Legs straight. My flesh rests easy in the hammock that is my bones. I am one with the night. The night is one with me.

Do I know that I'm asleep?

Color collides with color. Even with me in it, there is nothing wrong with my reality. Planets pass by. Stars shine their greetings. I am in the darkness. The darkness is in me. The darkness is everything. Visions are everywhere. Time is no more. There is no want. There is only tomorrow. Troubles were destroyed in the reclamation of dreams. I cannot go back. I'm too deep in prayer.

Do I know that I'm awake?

Noise flows. Voices interrupt. Pulled further from what is, I desperately grab hold of everything. I can't grab. I can only drag. The light gets closer and closer. The brilliance is extinguished. There is only a morbid glow. The artificialness of it all offers nothing. There is only the risk of opening the eyes. Divinity creeps in. Be near.

Do I know that I'm home?

Hands jostle me back to reality. Noise pulls my consciousness further from the dream. The sun is just coming up. I thought I was in reality. Every step draws me deeper into another dream. Each foot grows heavier as a new child climbs on. I go to work on the food. Every step opens up a new future. We are still asleep. Smells push us toward the table. Forks are our tools to partake of the sacrament.

Do I know that I'm at worship?

Clothes hide. Shoes disappear. Food falls to the ground. Screaming is the only chorus. Seats are dirty. Buckles won't snap. Each outfit looks like a robe. We are ready. Something has found us. We are one. I don't understand why we're going. We've already experienced everything out here. There is nothing to experience there. I can't imagine a reason to trade a more real reality for a less real reality. Divinity is bludgeoned to death verse by verse. Worship is the dying gasps of an irrelevant church. Community is an excuse to discuss divorce, disease and death. I'm just not interested. The kids moan. I drive. Beautiful words are exchanged. We keep pushing toward the service. I still can't figure out why we're going.

Do I know that I'm not a Christian?

Notes drop like sledgehammers. Words speak of days long played out. Dictionaries are a required part of the service. Even the hymnals are antiques. Worship was not important. Preservation was the order of the hour. Crayons filled the pew. Blue. Red. Green. Brown. Orange. Each hue reminded me of the morning. I colored. I didn't stop. I felt it in my bones. Salvation was in the crayons. The beauty of stacking colors on top of each other became apparent. I stacked until it was time to go. Looking at me after the service, the woman made a declaration, "If you didn't enjoy that music, you're not a Christian."

Do I know that I'm in the colors?

Find your seats. Beans spray. Rice flies. Payment declined. Forks land. Hurry and eat. Diapers changed. Time to go. Seats buckled. Air on. Drive again. Reality dances. Screaming. Shouting. Screaming.

Do I know that God is speaking?

Back to the dreams. Holding on. Something is out there. Pulling back. Eyes open. Colors jump out. Eyes closed. Deeper and deeper. Eyes open. Learning to breathe. Divinity is found in description of something other. Divinity is what was. God is what can be.

Do I know that I can be?

Group gathering. Judas is the topic. People talking. Community being shared. Jesus picked Judas. Surprise bubbles. Wrestling with God. Conversation is salvation. We are doing it.

Do I know salvation?

Eyes closed. Salvation is in the dreams. We experienced it all day today with our eyes open. Reality isn't real. Only the colors of the future can save us. See them.

Goodnight.

SEPTEMBER 1, 2016

Sidewalk Hate

"Faggot." Where did that come from? I politely smiled at the guy. I was just walking down the street. I was trying to be nice. How can a chance encounter become so hateful? I guess hate is the only answer. Though I've been called a "Faggot" before, this time was particularly painful. I think it hit me at a low moment. I grew angry. Then, I remembered an old adage I've used in sermons, "You can't love Jesus and hate your neighbor." Next time, I'm just going to choose the opposite of hate and simply say, "Thank you."

Amen.

SEPTEMBER 2, 2016

The One Question that Defines Our Faith

Does God experience our pain?

Amen.

SEPTEMBER 3, 2016

Problems.

Claiming a fictitious past. Finding a fictitious present. Praying for a fictitious future. You are the worst kind of liar. You don't remember when you're telling the truth. You say we have problems. Where were you? Where were you when the bodies dropped? Where were you when families were devastated? Where were you when the world went crazy? You were sitting on your swollen ass praying for your fictitious future. You are fiction in the midst of deadly realities. You speak of problems. You are the problem.

Amen.

SEPTEMBER 4, 2016

Listen. We keep hearing of pain and rumors of pain.

Think. Our society is often drowning. Our personal lives are sick. We need something more than what we can grasp to survive. Yet, we still reach.

Feel. Most people reach for connection. We assume that our identity will save us. We keep naming what we are. The problem is that the names are always partial. The identities are never complete.

Know. We are a blurred people. We have never been connected by our names or identities. We are connected by something much darker.

Search. We are a people united in despair. We find ourselves afraid. We find ourselves controlled by fear. We want safety. There is no safety. There is only God.

Ponder. The God who is with us. The God who experiences our pain. The God who is moving from despair to despair. The God who is searching for hope.

Find. Be. The God who is.

Amen.

SEPTEMBER 6, 2016

Those Confederate Flags in De Leon

Beauty reaches out and grabs you. I experience it every time. I see it. I feel it. I hear it. The land speaks. The fields sway. The sky never stops. I could go on and on. Make no mistake . . . De Leon is a beautiful place.

Unfortunately, everything turned ugly on our last visit. We were driving through town when we started seeing the Confederate flag everywhere. We saw the flag on houses. We saw the flag on businesses. We saw the flag on trucks. The stars and bars are unmistakable. The sting of the hate that accompanies the flag is too.

"Daddy . . . Why are they flying the hate flag?" Though we come from Confederate heritage, we're not interested in continuing or promoting the racism of the past. We teach our kids what the Confederate flag means. How could we not teach them to choose love over hate?

How does a town with so many churches have so many Confederate flags? I couldn't believe it. Was De Leon growing more racist with every visit? More than that, I suspected the town was becoming more fearful. The same scenario is repeatedly playing throughout our society.

The Violence of Being

There will be those who claim heritage. I don't buy it. If your heritage is important to you, you should be able to find less offensive ways of showing it. We all know that the Confederate flag has been a symbol of hate for a very long time. You don't need much knowledge of history to realize it.

As much as Jesus is talked about in De Leon, I invite you to follow him in loving all of your neighbors and tossing out those flags.

Rev. Dr. Jeff Hood
Denton, Texas

Amen.

SEPTEMBER 7, 2016

Dallas is Still in Denton

The slam of the car door sent me scrambling last night. I ran down the street as fast as I could. I knew it was happening all over again. Throughout my body, adrenaline exploded. The terror was back. When I finally stopped, I was alone. The dark streets of our neighborhood reminded me that I was still close to home.

"Get in!" I don't know that I've ever been more happy to see someone. For hours, I didn't where Emily was. We got separated after the shots. Everyone seemed to want to talk. "Dr. Hood will you pray with me?" "Rev. Hood do you have time for a brief interview?" "Dr. Hood, can I talk to you about what happened?" Though I talked to everybody, I just wanted to find Emily. The adrenaline seemed to be what was keeping me going. I did a live interview on WFAA. Emily saw me and knew where to pick me up. When we finally got on the highway to go toward Denton, I was ready to get home.

I slept three hours that night. Early the next morning, I was on Good Morning America. Immediately after that, I taped a segment for the CBS Evening News. The bright lights took their toll. For the next few days, the interviews didn't stop. I was exhausted. I still hadn't been able to deal with what was happening. Though I felt that it was important to share a message of love and justice, I wasn't prepared for the aftermath. Thousands of threats poured in. Our address was posted online. Eventually, Emily and our kids had to flee the area. Things slid out of control. After a phone call, the Denton Police Department arrived at our home.

The Violence of Being

"I just want you to know that I'm here to protect you." "Our job is to make sure nothing happens to your family." "We're not going anywhere until you're safe." Officers repeatedly reminded us that they were here to protect us. While the rhetoric in the struggle against police brutality is often that all officers are bad, I found the officers I encountered in Denton to be very gracious. Only a few days prior, I'd led one of North Texas' largest rallies of the year against police brutality right before a lunatic killed five officers. These officers had every reason to hate me. They didn't. I was constantly reminded that none of this was my fault. In the midst of the almost 9 days that we were under their protection, I'll never forget repeatedly being reminded of four words, "This is our home."

Two months after the tragedy, Dallas is still here. I think that might always be the case. Things have started to look slightly different. I cling to different. There is something salvific about different. Though I struggle to figure out where to go next, I know I have a home in Denton.

SEPTEMBER 22, 2016

Words for the Enough is Enough Rally

I apologize that I'm not with you this evening. Life won't allow it. So, I'm forced to communicate to you at this grave hour through the written word.

We are in the middle of a national crisis. The bodies keep dropping. The names keep piling up. What are we to do?

I don't believe there is anything we can do but pray. So, let our mouths cry out the prayer of freedom. So, let our feet stomp out the prayer of justice. So, let our hands clap out the prayer of change. Oh friends, this is the hour to move the entirety of our beings in prayer.

As our prayers meet at this perilous intersection of time and space, may we embody the transformation that we want to see in our world. Let's keep going my friends. Let's not stop until we arrive at that beautiful land called justice.

Amen.

SEPTEMBER 24, 2016

Staying Home: Churcholm Syndrome

Growing up, I was in church every Sunday. I sat in our favorite pew. I memorized every hymn. I remembered the scriptures. I sought Jesus the best I knew how. I always knew that something wasn't right about that space. Oppression came from every direction. I couldn't get out. I didn't know enough. Decades later, I sit here this morning with enough knowledge. I don't want to go to a traditional church for all the right reasons. Despite the tings I'm sure of, I'm still afraid to stay home.

About a year ago, I founded a house church that meets once per month in Fort Worth. We actually meet tonight. We are much more of a community than any traditional church I've ever attended. There are no favorite pews. We don't sing. Though we dabble in the scriptures, our experiences with God are usually the main topic of conversation. I don't have to seek Jesus in this space. Jesus is there before we ever get there. The beauty of it all is overwhelming. I have a church. So, why do I feel guilty for not going to a traditional church this morning when I'm going to our house church tonight?

I see it as a form of Stockholm Syndrome.

I have developed feelings of deep affection for my oppressor.

Maybe this is part of loving my oppressor?

Staying Home: Churcholm Syndrome

Maybe I even suffer from Churchholm Syndrome?

Regardless, I'm staying home this morning.

I know I'll experience church tonight.

Amen.

SEPTEMBER 25, 2016

Bart Ate God

"Where was God?" I knew the question was coming. I could feel it. My son is a smart kid. I knew he wouldn't let the death of an older former babysitter go without discussion. I welcome these questions. I don't hide from them. I engage them directly. So, I replied, "Bart ate God." Immediately, my son inquired, "Who is Bart?" Without hesitation, I offered, "Bart is a dinosaur that can teach us more about God than any book of scripture . . . because Bart is to blame for God's failure to show up and help again and again. Bart keeps God from doing God's work. This is what Bart looks like." The look on his face left no doubt, my son had never met a dinosaur like Bart before.

Amen.

SEPTEMBER 27, 2016

Dreams.

Eyes closed. Thoughts flood my brain. The deeper I fall asleep, the more the thoughts subside. Rapid-eye movement sets in. I'm lost in a world of dreams. There is one I've come to know well. Someone cries out. The police bust through the door. The officers point at me. I don't know what I've done it. I scream out that this is a misunderstanding. It doesn't matter. If they come to pick you up, you're guilty. The truth quickly becomes a very relative phenomenon. All they know is that they've found a body and they need to find the killer. Apparently, I fit the description. Under the weight of questioning, I cry out for a lawyer. The police make me sign a confession before I can see a lawyer. Why would an innocent man sign a confession? I'd been in that room over nine hours. Once the lawyer arrives, she explains that there is very little that she can do. Everyone wants to know why an innocent man would sign a confession. We proceed to trial. Even though I'm innocent, my lawyer basically leads me right into a death sentence. On multiple occasions, my attorney even fell asleep. I thought counsel was supposed to provide real counsel. I didn't get shit. I would have been better off defending myself. After I was taken to death row, I walked around my cell over and over. I can't get anyone to respond to my cries for help. Didn't anybody get my letters? The appeals aren't working. Everything seems to be happening so fast. I cry out to God for help. I'm ignored. By the time the day comes, I'm fresh out of prayers. I'd given God everything I got. When they strapped me to the gurney, I peed all over myself. Trembling as the needle press against my flesh and drew blood, I reached for one last prayer.

The Violence of Being

Looking to the windows, I cried out, 'I have no more prayers for God. I only know to pray to you. Before you kill me, will you consider doing what God would do.' After I said that, the execution proceeded much faster. I could feel the poison burning my insides. I felt like I was burning alive. I shoot up in my bed. Terrified, I grab some water. After calming down a bit, I try to consider what just happened. Even though I've dreamed the dream repeatedly, there is one idea that stays with me. Fresh out of prayers, the only thing we can do is ask people to do what God would do. I'm talking about the God of love not the God who commits genocide. For love so loved the world that love gave love's only begotten love that whosoever believes in love will not be executed in this life. I 'm ready for followers of God to start dreaming again about what it means to pray with your feet. Eyes close. Rapid-eye movement sets in. The colors draw me in. Dreams become reality and reality becomes dreams. The death penalty is no more. We finally realized what love was for.

SEPTEMBER 28, 2016

Prayer at the Conclusion of Shane Claiborne in North Texas

Let us pray-Oh God, we have participated in the mechanisms of death. We must repent before we approach you this evening with our requests. We are guilty of murder God. Please forgive us. (pause) The grace of God extends to the vilest of sinners. Let us proceed with the knowledge that our sins our forgiven. (pause) Friends, let us realize that we serve a God that declared the incarnation fully present in the lives of those who are in prison. Jesus is in prison. Jesus is on death row. Jesus is proceeding to the execution chamber. Jesus was crucified on a cross. Jesus was executed on a gurney. No matter the mechanism, Jesus was there . . . . Jesus died. We have killed our God. The only way to get our God back is to proceed to the place of death. Go to the chamber! God will meet you there. Don't spend a bunch of time talking strategy. Don't spend a bunch of time praying. Don't think about it. Go to the chamber! When you dare to go to the place where we killed our God, you will be changed. Our only hope of abolishing the death penalty is found in the chamber. Go to the chamber. God will meet you there.

Amen.

SEPTEMBER 30, 2016

Forgive Us Marksville: #JeremyMardis

Dear Marksville.

Though my activism has taken me to many places, I've never been to your town. For this, I'm profoundly sorry. I've kept up with the case of Jeremy Mardis ever since he was gunned down with his seatbelt on. Truth be known, I was too engaged in a variety of other cases to pay too much attention to this one. Judging by the lack of engagement from activists, I don't think I'm alone. I don't think time is the primary reason for the lack of engagement. The truth is plainer than that. When the victim is white and the perpetrators are black, no one wants to get excited about a case that bucks the national narrative. I find this to be disgusting. Doesn't an autistic child matter too?

God is with those who chant, "Black Lives Matter!" God is also with those who chant, "Jeremy's Life Matters!" We just have to be about proclaiming that life matters. I've watched the video of the murder multiple times. When I close my eyes, I can still see Jeremy's little body lying alone dead in the passenger seat. Let's make sure that that's the last time Jeremy Mardis ever lies alone again.

Rev. Dr. Jeff Hood
Denton, Texas

OCTOBER 2, 2016

The Last Person to Die for a Lie

Have you ever killed somebody? The question in and of itself is haunting. Have you ever killed somebody? Each word rattles my soul. Have you ever killed somebody? The more times I ask the question the more times I'm brought face to face with my own complicity in killing. Most people don't think about it like that. The more times I ask the question to others, the more times I get adamant denials of ever being involved in killing someone. Yet in the midst of a quickness to absolve ourselves of any sin, there is our death penalty. Each time the State of Texas kills someone, it's citizens are responsible. Since 1982, we have killed 537 people. Not only are we killers, we are serial killers. We are killing far more people than any other state. Not only are we serial killers, we are amongst the most prolific.

How did we get here? While it is always hard to pinpoint the beginning of any addiction, there is one particular reason that stands out. The State of Texas does it's killing at the Huntsville Unit in Huntsville, Texas. There's an area where protestors stand just outside the prison walls. I've stood out there many times and prayed for an end to executions. I don't have to ask about the reason for all of this. The truth is right in front of me. Just above the prison wall, a tall building arises with a cross on top. I've always been amazed that the State of Texas does it's killing so close to a cross. I guess I shouldn't been amazed. It's always been like that.

Didn't Jesus die for our sins? So, why do we need to keep on killing. People always wonder why the most Christian states execute the most people. I don't. When you believe that blood is necessary for the forgiveness of sin, it becomes easy to believe that people must die for their sins. At every execution, we are carrying out a modern ritual of atonement. Who receives the atonement? Who will forgive our sins? While I could talk more about the spiritual side of killing, I think the point is obvious. The Christianity that is practiced by most of the State of Texas only increases the body count.

How do you teach someone not to kill by killing? The death penalty is supposed to be a deterrent to killing. How could it be? The death penalty teaches people that there are ethical ways of killing. People committing murders are simply mimicking their government. We can't teach people how to stop killing by showing them how to do it again and again.

Killing is expensive. We know beyond a shadow of a doubt that is it more expensive to execute someone than put them in prison for the rest of their lives. Isn't killing always more expensive? Doesn't it weigh heavier on the soul?

What about the wrongfully executed? Out of the hundreds, there's got to be at least one. Was it Carlos De Luna? Was it Cameron Todd Willingham? Or was it someone else entirely?

I could go on and on.

There are so many reasons to abolish the death penalty. There is only one basic question that really matters: Are we better people after we execute someone? I can't imagine any possible scenario where the answer is yes. Killing always makes us worse. We can be better. We can stop killing.

I repent of killing.

I'm not alone.

Just last week, the Pew Research Forum released an article entitled, "Support for the death penalty lowest in four decades." I grabbed my heart and almost fell over when I read that headline. Though I've known that support for the death penalty has been declining for a number of years, this was the first time that I'd realized that it was at the lowest point it'd been at in almost four decades. Just under half of Americans now support the death penalty (49%), while 42% oppose it. Support is down from a high of 80% in 1994. Support has dropped 7% since March of last year. One mind changed at a time, the death penalty is dying.

Don't be the last person to kill for a lie.

OCTOBER 3, 2016

Denton Dinning with 5 Children

Children are always a surprise. No amount of planning can prepare you for when they come. I know Denton loves their festivals. So let me describe it like this, those first few months of life are like buying an unlimited pass to the festival of poop. We lost count of the poop sprays. The doctor told us that shotgun poop was a sign of good health. We left with no doubt that our children were the healthiest babies alive. We've all been told that Jesus is the Savior. I might have to disagree slightly. The worker at Chipotle who stepped in while I cleaned my child off is the Savior to me. There's something spiritual about caring for children. It's not the smells. It's the energy. When I returned, I asked the worker for forgiveness for the crisis. The worker absolved me of all my sins. After two shout outs to God, I started packing up. As I was buckling them into their seats, I got sprayed with vomit. I calmed down quickly. The worker ran outside with napkins to help me clean up again. Just like the Savior, the worker was right on time. I'm sure something else happened before we got home. Children are always a surprise.

"How do you do it?" We constantly hear this question. It's not that we have 5 children. Plenty of people have 5 children or even more. The difference is that we had 5 children in under 3 years. While we've been told that two sets of naturally occurring twins is unbelievably rare, we don't have much time to think about it. There are

Denton Dinning with 5 Children

5 children constantly demanding attention. There are 5 children in different stages of potty training. There are 5 children. While people often want to marvel at the process, we're just trying to get them fed.

Regularly, we find ourselves at Green Zatar. There is no kinder or gentler restaurant in Denton. Someone came up to our table and asked, "How do you do it?" I pointed to the workers. I don't know that I've known more kinder or gentler people ever. I wish I could say that about everywhere.

The dirty looks don't bother me. I figure that people are always rude about the things they don't understand. The direct comments can get rough. "You don't know how to wrap it up?" "You just didn't know when to stop?" "You're nuts!" I've heard these three comments recently at local restaurants. Guess where we're not going to eat? Who wants to go to a restaurant where people make these types of discriminatory comments, when you can go somewhere where you can get help? It truly does take a village. What kind of village is Denton? Is this the type of place where the village steps up for large families? I hope so. We're hungry.

+All 5 love Bahama Buck's.

OCTOBER 5, 2016

Voices of Love.

Have you ever heard voices? I hear them all. There are a particular set that are haunting. I hear them saying a variety of things. "I'm innocent." "Please God!" "Forgive me." "Why are you killing me?" The voices are too real to be fake.

I saw the horrible crime. Barney Fuller walked next door and killed his neighbors. I hear them too. "Please, don't kill for us." "God's love is enough." "Stop!" Even the victims know better than killing. Killing can't never avenge killing. Love is the only thing that can do that.

I can hear Barney Fuller praying. "Love be with those who kill." "Love be with those I killed." "Love be with me." May we learn to pray with him?

The execution of Barney Fuller is scheduled to begin on October 5, 2016 at 6pm.

Love still covers a multitude of sins.

Maybe love will save Barney Fuller.

Amen.

OCTOBER 5, 2016

Allahu Akhbar

I was surprised by the words. Since I'm not a Muslim, I'm not in places where people say "Allahu Akhbar" often. After the owner of an Iranian restuarant I frequent declared "Allahu Akhbar," he told me that was trying to remind me that God is greater. I was very moved. On the way home, I found myself repeatedly muttering,"Allahu Akhbar." I believe that God is greater. Don't you? This Sunday, I think every church should open worship with the powerful words, "Allahu Akhbar." It's about time that we remember that God is greater.

Amen.

OCTOBER 6, 2016

Missing Dreams

Have you ever missed a dream? You woke up before it started. You tried to catch it. It was gone. For the rest of your life, you're left to wonder about that dream. Dreams we meet in waking hours are like that too. We think that life can be better. We close our eyes. We miss it. We have to go where they are. We have to figure out how to catch the dreams.

Amen.

DECEMBER 12, 2016

The Absent God

The air was unusually cold for November. My nose was running and my eyes were watering. Nevertheless, I wanted to kiss her goodbye. I knocked on the back window. I could see her sitting in her chair. Slowly, she moved toward the sliding glass door. Eventually, we got it open. I gave her a hug and kissed her on the cheek. When we briefly saw some bad news on the television, my grandmother declared, "We're living in the end times." We went outside and I kissed her goodbye. That was the last time I ever saw her alive. A few weeks later, my grandmother died in her favorite chair. Though it's been two years, I still miss her. In her absence, I still feel the absence of God.

Yesterday, hundreds gathered in Uyo, Nigeria for the consecration of Akan Weeks at Reigners Bible Church International. People were excited for the chance to commune together. Not long after the church started, the metal church collapsed. Over 160 people died. As bodies stuck out from the rubble, God was absent.

Yesterday, people gathered in Cairo, Egypt to worship at a chapel connected to St. Mark's Cathedral. Mostly women and children squeezed in. In the midst of prayer, a bomb exploded. Bodies were littered throughout the building. In total, 25 people died. As blood flowed from the pews, God was absent.

Yesterday, people traveled to the stadium in Istanbul, Turkey to watch a football game. The announcers pumped up the crowd.

The Violence of Being

Cheers went up for each team. The beauty of sport was shattered when a car bomb exploded outside the stadium. A short time later, a suicide bomber detonated. 38 people died in the attacks. As people were torn apart, God was absent.

In all of these tragedies, God was absent. I believe my grandmother was right. We are living in the end times. We must declare the end of a benevolent God that is interested in our welfare. Judging from these tragedies, God has left us. God is absent from our pain. Perhaps in the end, God will find us again.

Amen.

DECEMBER 12, 2016

Christmas Everywhere

When we arrived home last night, we placed presents under the tree. The kids were really excited. After some persuading, we were able to get them to bed. Early this morning, we were awoken with shouts of, "It's Christmas!" We rushed downstairs to find all of the presents opened. Oscillating between frustration and laughter, I stopped to remember that Christmas is not defined by one day . . . Christmas is everywhere.

I wonder what it would be like for us to embrace the excitement of Christmas everyday. Though our kids were excited about presents, they have also been excited about the real meaning of Christmas. One of my sons asked me the other day, "Is Jesus going to come see us for Christmas?" I replied, "Jesus is everywhere." May we embrace the promise of everywhere every day.

Amen.

DECEMBER 13, 2016

War Crimes in Aleppo: Do Something!

I spent this morning watching videos from people in Aleppo. Person after person repeated the same message, I am going to die and this is going to be my last video. People are being slaughtered in the streets. Blood runs down the sidewalk. People can't get out. In the midst of unbelievable suffering, the regime of Bashar al-Assad keeps killing. What are we to do?

When these atrocities take place, I often hear people talk about their inability to do anything. Unable to figure anything out, people choose to sit in front of a screen and watch events play out. Surely, this is not the solution. There is an answer to such questions. Paul calls to us from Philippians 2:17, "Your faith makes you offer your lives as a sacrifice in serving God." Do we have faith? We are called to give our lives to stop these atrocities.

Should we go to Aleppo and die? If we are able, we are absolutely called to lay down our lives. If not, then we should give our lives to stopping this atrocity from right where we are. Certainly, Jesus calls us to go deeper than our screens. God has not damned the people of Aleppo, but may God damn us if we fail to act at this crucial moment.

Amen.

DECEMBER 13, 2016

His Name is Francisco Serna

On Monday night, a 73-year-old grandfather suffering from dementia named Francisco Serna made a lethal decision . . . he decided to go for an evening walk. Somewhere near the 7900 block of Silver Birch Avenue, Serna came in contact with a police officer. Thinking he had a gun, the officer shot Serna 9 times. After the incident, no gun was found.

Where was God in the midst of such tragedy? I believe that God was right there with Francisco Serna. I believe that God took every shot and bled out. However, the bigger question is: Where were we?

Amen.

DECEMBER 14, 2016

The Death of Truth

Throughout the last few months, numerous leaders in our country have made wild claims that have been proven to have no grounding in reality. There is also the proliferation of fake news that has motivated numerous people to do a variety of things. All around us untruths are taken as fact. Those who challenge these claims are considered dangerous enemies worthy of violent reprisals. Take the case of Edgar Welch. After reading a fake news story claiming that Hillary Clinton was running a child molestation ring out of a Washington, D.C. pizza restaurant named Comet Ping Pong, Welch traveled from North Carolina to D.C. to investigate with an assault rifle and ended up firing a shot inside the restaurant. Even though restaurant owners repeatedly repudiated the fake news story, Welch clung to the fake news. This phenomenon is taking place all over our society. Truth is dead.

Untruths cannot go unchallenged. There is great danger in our current state. In a world of shifting shadows, the resurrection of truth begins with demanding the truth. We are the resistance. We cannot continue to be imprisoned by twisted words and concepts. In the words of John 8:32, may we " . . . know the truth, and allow the truth to set us free."

Amen.

DECEMBER 15, 2016

Pray for Dylann Roof

Earlier today, a jury found Dylann Roof guilty of killing 9 people at the Mother Emanuel African Methodist Episcopal Church. An avowed white supremacist, Roof admitted that he killed the churchgoers because they were black. Seeking to ignite a race war, Roof wanted to be a savior for white people. Now, the punishment phase of the trial will determine whether or not Roof faces the death penalty.

For the first few months, I prayed daily for the victims and their families of the Mother Emmanuel shooting. On a regular basis, I still do. The shooting left a deep impression on my soul. I couldn't fathom how anyone could commit such an atrocity. In the midst of my confusion, I turned to God. Over time, I felt the need to pray for Dylann Roof. At first, I resisted. How could I pray for someone so evil? After much prayer, I realized that Roof was a child of God and as worthy of prayer as any child of God. I started praying for Roof. I'm especially praying right now.

Soon, a jury will soon decide whether or not to sentence Dylann Roof to death. All followers of Jesus should join me in prayer. We cannot love our neighbor as our self and kill them. The words of Jesus are just as poignant now as they were back then. You can't follow Jesus and be about killing. The death penalty is contrary to everything followers of Jesus believe. We have to pray for the killing to stop.

Pray for Dylann Roof.

Amen.

DECEMBER 16, 2016

The God Beyond God

"The God Beyond God." Paul Tillich's infamous conception of God has long marinated in my heart. I've dreamed of the God beyond religion and occasionally touched something more. Tillich is not alone in his estimations of God. In 36:26, Job declares, "Surely God is great, and we do not know him . . . " The unknowability of God is an important part of true faith. If we were to have complete knowledge of God, there would be no reason for belief . . . we would just know God.

Until we meet God, we will only have very limited partial knowledge. Eventually, we will encounter the God beyond words. We will touch the God beyond our religions. There is no reason to quibble over religion. We are all seeking the God beyond God. Put down your words and believe.

Amen.

DECEMBER 17, 2016

Born to Be Murdered? : A Word from Bethlehem

The Christmas season always makes me ponder a pivotal question. Did God send Jesus to die? I'm not talking about a death of natural causes. I'm talking about a brutal painful death. I'm talking about a bloody murder. Did God know about the suffering that was to come? If God knows everything, as traditional Christian doctrine teaches, then the answer is yes. God sent Jesus to take the crown of thorns. God sent Jesus to be beaten to the point of death. God sent Jesus to be crucified. God sent Jesus to be abused. What type of God would do such a thing? Would you send your child to endure such suffering? Can you imagine rejoicing over your child in Bethlehem when you know what brutalization is coming? If traditional Christian doctrine is to be believed, God is the greatest child abuser of them all. I simply can't believe in a God like that. I choose to believe that the baby in Bethlehem represented the best of who God was and is. I choose to reject traditional doctrine. I choose to believe there is another way.

God did not kill Jesus. God didn't know what was coming. God only knew the hope of the baby. God sent Jesus on a rescue mission to save the world with no idea if it was going to work. I don't think this is just wishful thinking. I think it is the only plausible way to think about a righteous God. God has to be ignorant of what is to come. I think there is biblical evidence for such belief. Matthew 27:19 reads, "While Pilate was sitting in the judgment hall, his wife sent him a message: 'Have nothing to do with that innocent man, because in a dream last night, I suffered much last night.'" As Pilate was about to condemn Jesus, his wife begs him to stop. I see this moment as one of God's last attempts to save Jesus. God cannot be held responsible for the murder of Jesus because God didn't know. God sent the baby in Bethlehem to bring hope not to be murdered. God had no idea what was going to happen. God kept trying to save Jesus. That's why God led Mary and Joseph to the stable. God is not the great child abuser of all. We are.

Amen.

DECEMBER 19, 2016

Murder in Ankara :
The Perpetual Crucifixion

Earlier today, Turkish police officer Melvut Mert Altinua walked into an art exhibition in Ankara and perused the art. A few minutes after Russian Ambassador Andrey Karlov started speaking about Turkish-Russian relations, Altinua fired multiple shots that sliced through Karlov's body. Frantically waving a gun, Altunua gave praise to Allah and declared, "Do not forget Aleppo!" The Russian government has been extremely instrumental in defending the regime of Syrian President Bashar al-Assad. The entire shooting was captured on video. I watched it this afternoon.

Early in the video, I felt sick to my stomach Melvut Mert Altinua approached Andrey Karlov from behind. The moments are incredibly ominous. Then, I saw the bullets blow through the shirt of Karlov. In the midst of it all, I couldn't help but think about the passion of Christ. I believe that Jesus is with all who are murdered. When someone is shot down, I believe that Jesus is shot down too. Jesus is the God of the continuous incarnation. So, it also makes sense that Jesus was also with Altinua when he was later killed by Turkish special forces. The incarnation brings us together by taking our shots. Jesus lives the perpetual crucifixion.

Amen.

DECEMBER 23, 2016

Forbidden Words: Christmas Interactions with the Queer Christ

An Interpretation of the Christmas Story

In the days of Texas Governor Greg Abbott, there was an old minister named Bob whose partner was named Tommy. For many years, the couple had wanted a child and now they were old. One evening as Bob was alone praying for a child, a bright light came over him. Standing and turning, Bob tried to run away. The light would not let Bob go. In that moment, the light began to speak, "I love you. You do not have to be afraid. I want you to know that you are about to adopt a child and her name will be John. She will bring good news of salvation and liberation to the world. The child will be queer beyond imagination and filled with the Spirit of God." Bob couldn't believe what he was hearing, "How will I know that this is true? Don't lie to us. We are too old." The light responded, "I am Gabby and I stand in the presence of a God that is queer beyond your wildest imagination. I have been sent to tell you that the queerness that flows from our God will fill up your daughter John. To make the situation queerer, I have been told to take away your power to speak until the day these events transpire."

When the light appeared, the doors slammed shut and the windows closed to lock Bob in. Tommy heard all of the commotion and ran downstairs. The neighbors heard everything and rushed to help. After some time, the door slowly opened. Bob walked out with a really intense tan and covered in glitter. Everyone tried to ask him what happened, but Bob couldn't speak. Tommy ran a tablet over and Bob typed out that a daughter named John was on her way. The two men embraced and jumped up and down. The neighbors couldn't figure out what was going on and decided that the couple must have really lost it this time.

After a few months of nesting in faith, a Child Protective Services (CPS) agent named Marina called to ask Tommy if they would be interested in adopting a little girl named John. Although the child did not meet any of the identity criteria the couple had previously and perhaps selfishly asked for, Marina thought she would try. Bob knew that he had heard the voice of God and this was the child of their dreams. Marina was shocked when Tommy replied with an emphatic "YES!" for both of them. She was even scared to tell them that it was still going to be some time before their little girl John would arrive. However, nothing could dampen Tommy and Bob's excitement. Tommy told Marina they would wait forever.

Months later, Gabby was sent by God to a queer woman named Mary in a town called Dallas. While Mary's partner Josie was at work, Gabby appeared to her in a great light, "Hello! God is with you." Mary was deeply perplexed.

Gabby replied, "Do not be afraid. You are chosen by God to conceive in your womb a child named Jesus. The child will be the child of God who shows the world the power of love." Mary immediately replied, "How can this be, I only sleep with my partner Josie?" Gabby replied, "The Spirit of the Queer will come upon you. The love of God will overwhelm you. The child will be queer. The child will be the perfect Queer of God. And even right now in their old age, your cousin Tommy and his partner Bob have a daughter named John they are going to adopt. Know that nothing is impossible with God." Mary fell to the feet of Gabby and declared, "I love the Queer and I will do whatever God asks of me, may your words be accomplished and more." Gabby dissolved in front of her.

A few days later, Mary went up to Denton. She went directly to Bob and Tommy's house. Mary met Tommy in the driveway and greeted him with a loud shriek of excitement. Right after a collective embrace, the phone rang. Tommy picked up the line and Marina asked if he would briefly like to hear John for the first time. On the other end of the phone, Tommy could hear a little baby cooing and he began to cry tears of joy. Then Tommy was filled with the Spirit of God and he cried aloud, "Mary you are indeed carrying God! The fruit of your womb will be the queering of all nations. Who am I, that the carrier of the Queer shall visit me? Did you see that? As soon as you walked up, I got to talk to my little daughter John for the first time. That was no accident. You brought God into this space. I know that the promise of God, the promise of the Queer is going to be fulfilled in you."

And Mary said: "My soul rejoices in the queerness that I have found. For my God has found me. I rejoice in the savior of my life. I rejoice in the Queer. I am so unworthy of a miracle of God, yet God dwells in me. From this day forth generations will count me queer, so wonderful is this God-granted discovery. Praise be to the creator of queerness. God's name is Queer. The queerness of God endures from generation to generation. The keepers of normativity will be restored to their queerness. The hungry and poor will never want again. God will stand on the side of the Queer forever."

Mary stayed with Tommy for about 2 weeks and then returned home.

Not too long after, the time came for Tommy and Bob's daughter John to arrive. The entire community knew how much the couple wanted a child and rejoiced to God with flowing champagne. Unfortunately, Bob was still unable to speak.

When it came time to baptize the child, many tried to ask Tommy if he and Bob wanted to change the name of the child. "Don't you know that she won't know her gender identity if you name her John? Plus, who exactly are you naming the child after?" The group gathered for the baptism motioned for Bob and asked him one last time about the child's name. Bob typed out on his tablet, "Her name is John!" All were amazed. Immediately, as he displayed the tablet, Bob's tongue was loosened and he began to speak, praising God. This queer series of events scared the shit out of all of Denton. Everyone wondered, "How did Bob lose and gain his ability to speak? If this child is chosen queer by God, what will the child become?" There was no question that the hand of God was upon them.

Then Bob began to speak words of justice and peace, "God loves us. God has redeemed us. God has raised for us a queer savior. God will save us from the keepers of normativity and make us queer. God is unfailing in God's love and you my daughter John will be called the prophet of the Most Queer, for you will go before God to prepare God's way and give knowledge of salvation to all people. The queerness of God will dawn on us, to give light to all who dwell in darkness and death, to guide us to the place of peace."

John grew and became strong in spirit, and she was in the wilderness of Denton until the day she appeared publicly in Dallas.

While Mary was incredibly excited about the coming of baby Jesus, Josie couldn't figure out what was going on. Regardless of Mary's story, Josie felt like Mary must have cheated on her with a man. Now, Josie felt unsure of Mary's sexuality or basic identity. Josie decided it would be best to break up with Mary privately, as she was not interested in having a dramatic public break up. Not long after Josie made her final decision, she fell asleep and began to dream. A bright light appeared to Josie and said, "Do not be afraid to take Mary as your wife forever, for the child conceived in her is from the Spirit of God. She will bear a queer child and you are to name the child Jesus, for Jesus will show the world the danger of normativity. The child shall also be called Emmanuel or 'God is with us.' Now, go and make her your wife."

Mary and Josie were married soon after.

During that time, President Barack Obama sent out an executive order stating that the entire nation should register. This was the healthcare registration and was taken while Greg Abbott was Governor of Texas. So all citizens went to their hometowns to be registered. Since marriage was difficult in Texas, a pregnant Mary had to take the chance of ignoring the decree for legally unmarried persons to go to their hometowns and followed her wife Josie on her journey from Dallas to the town of Cooper Creek, because Josie descended from the Coopers. Feeling vulnerable and longing to be married, Mary and Josie went into town to get married before the baby Jesus was to be born.

At the clerk's office, Mary and Josie were treated poorly. Mary felt a tremendous amount of pressure in the lobby and her water broke. The baby was coming quickly. Mary and Josie raced out of the building and sought a place for Mary to have the child. After being rejected at the hospital due to a lack of insurance, Josie tried to get a room at the one hotel in Cooper Creek. The hotel manager said that the hotel didn't usually allow lesbians, but that he would open his barn to the couple for free. Upon arrival to the barn, Mary collapsed with loud cries and Josie helped deliver the child.

Right outside of Cooper Creek, there were migrant farm workers living in the fields, keeping watch over their crops by night. Then an angel appeared in the sky and light filled everything. The migrant farm workers were terrified. The angel said to them, "Do not be afraid. I am bringing you good news of great joy. Tonight, for you is born a savior in the city of Cooper Creek. This is how you will find the child . . . let the spirit guide you to a child wrapped in cloth in a manger." Then all of a sudden, thousands of angels filled the sky praising love and declaring, "Glory to God in the highest and peace and goodwill to all." When the angels departed, the sky returned to dark. The migrant farm workers looked at each other and said in unison, "Let's go and see this miracle that God has revealed to us." Running, the migrant farm workers found the baby lying in the manger.

Mary and Josie were holding each other next to the manger. By this time, some kind hotel workers had arrived to try and help. The migrant farm workers recounted all that they had seen and the gathered people were amazed. Mary silently pondered all the beauty in her heart. The migrant farm workers returned to the fields glorifying and praising God for all they had experienced.

After eight days, Mary and Josie decided to baptize the child. The migrant farm workers joined Mary and Josie at a small creek. This was the only space available to them. A radical local minister poured water over the child's head and declared his name Jesus. The gathered cheered the queer events.

Mary had to heal a bit before they were able to travel for the dedication. When the time came, Mary, Josie, and Jesus traveled to Dallas. Upon arrival, they went to the Cathedral for Jesus' dedication. Outside the Cathedral, there was an older homeless gentleman named Simeon. Many years prior, Simeon had a vision while in a drug-induced stupor. God told Simeon that he would not die until he met the Messiah. Guided by the Spirit of God, Simeon tried to enter the Cathedral. Unfortunately, suspecting Simeon of being a drunken panhandler, some of the hired security guards would not let him in. God told Simeon to go to the side door of the Cathedral. When Mary and Josie brought Jesus forward to be dedicated, Simeon took hold of the child to the surprise of everyone. The security guards tried to rush Simeon, but, sensing the Spirit of God at work, Mary called them off.

Praising God, Simeon declared, "Savior, you may now dismiss your servant in peace. Mine eyes have seen your queerness and know that your salvation is the salvation of all people. I have waited my whole life to hold this child."

Mary and Josie were amazed at the events that were transpiring. Simeon blessed them and declared, "This child will be the liberation of all. The queerness of many will be revealed, especially in you."

As Simeon finished speaking, an old bag lady named Anna stood and began to praise the child. Anna had lived in the Cathedral for many years, praying day and night.

"Jesus is the redemption of all people and in this queer we will all find our queerness."

Mary, Josie, and Jesus left the Cathedral and made the journey to Ponder, the place they had chosen to settle down.

A few years later, monks from Asia showed up in Dallas, "Where is this queer child who has been born to be ruler of all nations? We observed the star in the sky and wanted to pay homage." When Governor Greg Abbott heard about this, he was frightened, and all the powerful elites of Texas with him; and calling together all of the religious leaders, he inquired of them where the Messiah was to be born. They told him, "The child was born in Cooper Creek." Then Governor Abbott called in the monks and learned from them the exact time that the star had appeared. The Governor then sent the monks to Cooper Creek and said, "When you find the child, send me word and I will come pay homage to the child." The monks left and continued to follow the star until it stopped over the place where Jesus was. On entering the apartment, they saw the child with Mary and they knelt down to worship. Then, opening their suitcases, they offered the child gifts of gold, frankincense, and myrrh. The beauty of the moment was overwhelming for all involved. After a night of celebration and drinking with Mary and Josie, the monks went to sleep on a blow up mattress in the living room. In their sleep, God spoke to them and warned them not to return to Governor Abbott. The next morning, after saying goodbye and encouraging Mary, Josie, and Jesus to be careful, the monks evaded the Governor and traveled to Oklahoma City and flew through Canada back to Asia.

A few nights after the visit of the monks, an angel appeared to Josie in a dream and said, "Get up and take Mary and Jesus to Mexico. Remain there until I tell you that it is safe to come back. For Abbott is going to imprison every child in Texas he thinks might look like Jesus and try to destroy their spirits in the Texas Prison Industrial Complex." Josie, Mary, and Jesus left immediately and made it to the border of Mexico by morning. Not having any identification, Josie and Mary bought water at a gas station and traveled through the desert, taking turns holding Jesus on their backs. The family settled in Monterrey. This fulfilled the prophecy, "Out of Mexico I have called my child."

When Governor Abbott realized that the monks had tricked him, he became enraged. The Governor imprisoned all children that he thought might look like Jesus. Governor Abbott stole the lives of these children. Most of the state didn't seem to care or notice, as Abbott consistently imprisoned and executed innocent people. This fulfilled the prophecy, "The unquieted tears of mothers will reveal the injustice of the system."

When Governor Abbott left office, an angel appeared to Josie and said, "It is now safe for you to return to Texas." Josie, Mary, and Jesus were denied entrance at the border, due to their lack of documentation. So once again, the family had to make the dangerous trip through the desert. Exhausted, the family arrived in Brownwood and spent the night, before returning to North Texas. Josie had a dream that warned him to avoid Dallas, because there was a mayor there who refused to support queer families. In turn, Mary,

The Violence of Being

Josie, and Jesus went to Ponder, Texas. The prophets words were fulfilled, "He will be called a Ponderian."

Jesus grew queerer with each passing moment.

Today, the miracle of queerness still lives and the dream of a world made queer will never die.

Amen.

DECEMBER 26, 2016

The End of Memory is The Beginning of God

On Christmas Day, I spent time with my grandmother. We've always been close, but this year she didn't even know who I was. Dementia has taken all of her memories. At one point, I looked over and saw my grandmother talking to a plastic bag. I scooted over to hear what she was saying. When I got close enough, I heard, "God, I didn't realize you were going to make it today." Initially, I laughed at the absurdity of the conversation. Then, I realized that I was the one being absurd. My grandmother has lost all her memories and yet believes in the presence of God far more than I do. We think our memories are so important. We cling to them with all that we are. Perhaps, we have been clinging to the wrong thing. Perhaps, the end of memory is the beginning of God.

Amen.

DECEMBER 30, 2016

Is the Slaughter of the Innocent the Slaughter of God?

In the midst of their journey to meet the child of God, the wise folks stopped by to see King Herod. Pretending to be excited about the birth, Herod asks the wise folks to come back by and tell him where the child is so that he might exalt the child. Herod was afraid that the child would rise up and challenge his rule. After meeting Jesus, the wise folks were warned to not go back to Herod. When he realized that he had been tricked, Herod decided to slaughter every child under the age of two in Bethlehem. In the midst of coming danger, God warns Mary and Joseph to take Jesus and flee to Egypt. Upon arrival, the family was safe. Back in Bethlehem, blood ran down the streets.

This story raises key questions about who we believe God to be. Was Jesus worth the cost of all the dead children? Maybe we should ask the parents of all the children whose kids were murdered. Why didn't God stop the slaughter? God warned Joseph and Mary to flee to Egypt. Why didn't God warn everyone else? These children were innocent and God allowed them to be slaughtered. Is this a God worth believing in? Maybe the slaughter of the innocent is the slaughter of our ideas about God. God does not seem to be capable of stopping the slaughter. Either God was incapable or God is the cruelest being to ever exist. I choose to believe that God was and is incapable. I choose to believe that God didn't know what was going to happen. I am comfortable with a God that doesn't know. I am not comfortable with a God who knew and did nothing. The problem with thinking that God was incapable is that God seems to know enough to warn everyone that God wants to warn. Maybe there were other warnings too. Maybe others simply chose not to leave. When Herod gave the command, there were plenty of children to kill. It seems that Mary, Joseph and Jesus are the only ones to leave. In the midst of an age of terror, maybe God was the original terrorist. Would God allow our children to be slaughtered? Many children are. Despite the fact that the Biblical evidence seems to point to a dastardlier conclusion, I choose to believe that God is always doing the best God can. Perhaps, I choose wrongly.

Amen.

www.ingramcontent.com/pod-product-compliance
Lightning Source LLC
Chambersburg PA
CBHW071426150426
43191CB00008B/1058